ARTISANS

GLASS

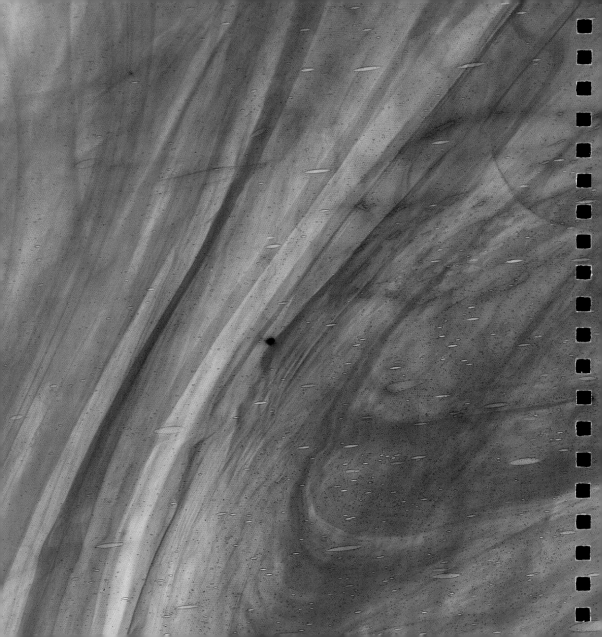

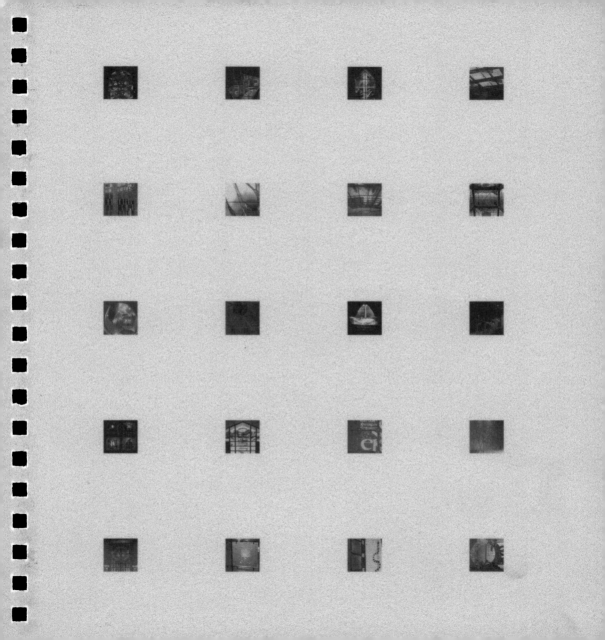

ARTISANS

GLASS

AN INSPIRATIONAL PORTFOLIO

JERA MAY MORTON

Watson-Guptill Publications
New York

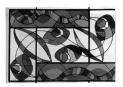

First published in the United States in 1999
by Watson-Guptill Publications,
a division of BPI Communications, Inc.,
1515 Broadway, New York, NY 10036

Art Director: Peter Bridgewater
Editorial Director: Sophie Collins
Designer: Alan Osbahr
Project Editor: Nicola Young
Editor: Lindsay McTeague
Page layout: Alan Osbahr
Photography: Richard Waite
Picture research: Vanessa Fletcher

Library of Congress Catalog Card Number:
98-89047

ISBN 0-8230-0305-1

This book was conceived, designed,
produced, and first published
in the United Kingdom in 1999
by THE IVY PRESS LIMITED
2/3 St Andrews Place
Lewes, East Sussex BN7 1UP

Reproduction and Printing in Hong Kong by
Hong Kong Graphic and Printing Ltd.,
(photo: Jon Lewis, *Swish Window*)

CONTENTS

INTRODUCTION

Glass has a fascinating

history that can be traced right

back to the antiquity of the

Middle East. In this section the

history of glassmaking is explored,

from the revolutionary discovery of

glass blowing at the end of the first

century B.C. *to its continuing*

popularity today.

*Harbour Lights
Cinema
Enameled glass
wall, Southampton,
England.
Martin Donlin*

From vast architectural projects to small-scale decorative mirrors, from
traditional celestial windows to abstract sculpture, contemporary stained
glass, or the more modern term, architectural glass, embrace such a
diversity of art forms it can be hard to consider them merely as one
discipline. Yet all these art forms are linked through common techniques
and the versatile and challenging medium of glass.

Within this book a portfolio of work from a cross section of
international artists illustrates the tremendous scope in which architectural
glass is used today. An example of each artist's work is shown and is
accompanied by a profile, based on the artist's own words, detailing
how each approaches and executes his or her work. This gallery of
contemporary work is preceded by an introduction to the history of the
medium and an insight into the range of traditional and contemporary
materials and techniques used.

Working with glass first began thousands of years ago in the
Middle East, where glass was valued as highly as precious stones.
Artisans in Egypt and Mesopotamia used heat to transform natural
materials such as sand (in the form of silica), seaweed (soda ash),
brushwood (potash), and lime into a beautiful substance with diverse
qualities. By adapting metal-casting and ceramic techniques these
craftsmen created beads of glass to imitate jewels and, later, around
1500 B.C., developed their skills to produce small perfume bottles,
cosmetic jars, tableware, inlays, and the first window panes.

A range of casting methods was used. One of the simpler
techniques involved pouring molten glass into a shallow open mold
and then allowing the glass to cool gradually, or anneal. A more
complicated method used interlocking molds, which were filled with
fragments of glass or glass rods and fired in a kiln to create small

vessels. With the core-forming technique—an alternative method commonly used for forming vessels—a mixture of clay, sand, and dung was manipulated into the desired shape around a metal rod. This was then dipped into a crucible of molten glass, or wound with threads of glass, creating a pattern of woven colors.

New Discoveries

These ancient methods continued until, toward the end of the first century B.C., the Phoenicians found that glass could be blown by mouth. The discovery that a bubble of molten glass could be expanded, elongated, and manipulated into almost any shape, blown into a mold or spun out into a flat disk, revolutionized the art of glass-making and was a key ingredient in the subsequent development of stained glass. Mouth-blown glass—in contrast to the highly colored, opaque, and stonelike kiln-formed glass—brought out the translucent, light-transmitting qualities of the medium, and the early Romans, who had previously used thin sheets of alabaster for some of their more prestigious windows, began to use colored glass set into a framework of wood or bronze.

Although the Romans take the credit for being the first to make glass large enough for windows, the full glory of stained glass was not reached until the Middle Ages, when it prospered under the patronage of the Church. Stained glass was born out of a fusion of glass chemistry and the techniques of glass-blowing with enameling and metalwork, and influenced in style by illuminated manuscripts, mosaics, and frescoes. Set in stupendous medieval—particularly Gothic—architecture, stained glass, with its depth of color and ability to transmit light from the outside world, provided the perfect vehicle to illustrate the stories of the Christian faith. Glass windows are known to have existed in churches as early as the

sixth century A.D., but the golden age was during the thirteenth and
fourteenth centuries in the great churches and cathedrals of Europe.
These vast translucent windows filled the sacred buildings with glorious
rays of colored light, creating an inspiring and spiritual atmosphere.

Technological Developments

From the fifteenth to the nineteenth centuries, many changes took place
in the development of stained glass. Glass painting became more
sophisticated and paler colors were used, bringing more light and less
intensity of color into churches. As the Renaissance flourished, medieval
glass became unfashionable and there was a surge in enameling and
panel painting. Painted glass, along with heraldic glass and realistic
portraits heavily painted with opaque enamels onto white glass, became
popular in private residences and public buildings. This style of work
continued until the mid-nineteenth century, when influence from the Arts
and Crafts Movement and the revival in Gothic architecture reawakened
interest in medieval stained glass and old techniques were rediscovered.
Toward the end of the century, American painters John La Farge and
Louis Comfort Tiffany had a great influence on stained glass. Working
independently, they conducted numerous experiments and created
endless grades of color, texture, and brilliance in the glass, taking
commissions from churches and private houses. The colors of stained
glass had been restored.

Throughout history some of the more dramatic changes in the
style and use of stained glass have been driven by technological
developments. One of the most significant was the invention, in the mid-
twentieth century, of the float process, in which continuous sheets of
glass can be mechanically produced by floating hot glass onto a bed of

molten tin. For the first time, large sheets could be made cheaply and efficiently, with precision accuracy, and consequently they soon became a major building material. The availability of new materials, together with the birth of studio glass in the late 1950s and the subsequent use of glass as an artistic medium, has contributed to the increasing number of individual artists working with architectural glass.

Glassmaking into the Millennium

The use of stained glass is now well established in modern architecture, with stunning results. From the outside, external walls can act as frames to giant windows of color and texture. On the inside of a building, glass is the source of daylight, so consequently it has a tremendous influence on the inner space. Its endless colors and qualities, ranging from total opacity to complete clarity, can be used to produce just the right atmosphere and mood to suit the function of the building. Its translucency, for instance, makes it an excellent material for interior room dividers and screens to separate areas while still retaining a feeling of openness and space.

In addition to architectural and ecclesiastical works, there has been a dramatic expansion in the application of stained glass in a multitude of other fields, including sculpture, furniture, and the public arts. Many artists who principally work in other fields, such as textile artists or painters, have diversified into glass for specific projects and, similarly, artists who usually work in glass often combine it with other artistic media. This increasing fusion of glass with other art forms and materials, together with the constant advances in glass technology, continues to broaden the potential of this ancient substance, driving it forward as a thriving contemporary medium.

MATERIALS

Many different types of glass are

used to create works in

contemporary stained glass,

including antique glass, crown

glass, and float glass. This section

examines these and other forms of

glass, how they are made, and

what they are used for. Traditional

stained glass materials such as lead

and essential tools of the craft are

also discussed.

An artist selects
the right texture and
shade of antique
glass for his work

GLASS

ANTIQUE GLASS

One of the mouth-blown glasses that is specifically made for the manufacture of stained glass is known as antique glass. Flat sheets are produced, firstly by blowing a paraison, or small bubble of molten glass, which is repeatedly blown larger, reheated, and then swung to elongate it into a long cylindrical bubble. Once the bubble has cooled, the ends are cracked off to make an open cylinder called a muff. A glass cutter is used to score along the length of the cylinder, and it is then put into a spreading kiln. The heat causes the glass to relax and open along the line of the fracture, and a "flattener" who works at the mouth of the kiln smooths the glass out with a wooden batlike tool in order to create the required flat sheet.

A striking feature of antique glass is its vivid color. Countless shades are possible, obtained by adding varying quantities of metal oxides to a batch of clear glass. Different metals yield different colors: copper and chromium make blue-green; cobalt creates blue; sodium, cadmium, and gold give oranges, yellows, and ruby reds. If the resulting glass is of a uniform, solid color it is referred to as pot metal; if it consists of a clear or tinted glass coated with one or more layers of glass of a contrasting color it is known as flashed glass. When light passes through a double- or triple-colored flash, the different colors merge into one tone. Sandblasting and acid-etching techniques are frequently used on flashed glass to remove the surface color in parts, revealing the base glass beneath.

The radiant colors and beautifully rich tones of antique glass are often complemented by irregular patterns and surface textures. These characteristic imperfections in the glass are created by deliberately modifying the blowing techniques in order to produce interesting striated markings, colored streaks, and bubbles, all of which contribute to the distinctive and unique quality of mouth-blown glass.

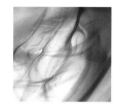

Antique glass comes in a variety of striking colors. Here, several different types, including cylinders, are shown prior to being flattened into sheets *(left)*. Mouth-blown glass is alive with its own textures, streaks, and bubbles *(below)*.

A roundel of crown glass is spun at the glory hole *(right)*. The blown roundel is spun on the iron and shaped using a wooden batten *(above)*.

CROWN GLASS

A traditional mouth-blowing technique, similar to that used for antique glass, is employed to make crown glass. A large bubble is blown, opened at one end, and manipulated into a bowllike shape. This is repeatedly reheated and spun vigorously until it flares out into a flat disk, or roundel, which can be over a yard in diameter. It is then cracked off the blowing iron and placed in a lehr—a special cooling kiln.

The lehr allows the glass to anneal—cool down gradually—which is necessary to prevent the glass from cracking. Once the disk has annealed, panes of glass can be cut from the flattest part and used for glazing. The center of the disk has a characteristic swirl where the iron was attached. In the seventeenth and eighteenth centuries, this part of the disk—known as bull's eye or bullion glass—was cheaper because of its thick, irregular form and was commonly used in the homes of poorer people, public houses, and farm buildings.

Crown glass can be clear or—if different types of colored glass are added during the first stages of blowing—solid-colored, translucent, or multicolored. The techniques for making crown glass were known to the Romans and were employed later by craftsmen in the magnificent stained-glass windows of the twelfth to fourteenth centuries. Today, crown glass is much less common, more of a specialty glass for individual artists wanting to create specific colors and patterns.

The romantically named Norman slab glass was developed in the nineteenth century specifically for stained glass. It is made by blowing a balloon of glass into a vertical rectangular mold. The narrow top of the bubble is cracked off, leaving a rectangular box that, when sharply tapped at the corners, breaks into four small rectangular panes and one square pane. Each piece tends to be thicker, and therefore darker, in the middle, and thinner and lighter toward the edges. Although beautiful, Norman slab is difficult to work with because it is hard to fix into lead and its varying thickness can cause internal stresses if the glass is fired.

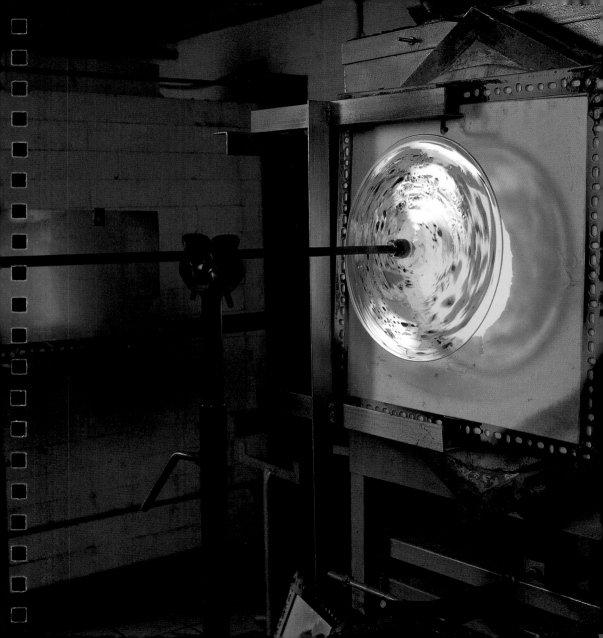

FLOAT GLASS

The British company Pilkington Brothers invented float glass soon after World War II. This discovery revolutionized architecture and the glass industry, turning glass into an inexpensive and versatile building material. Before this, sheet glass was made by pouring molten glass onto a flat surface, smoothing it out with a roller, and then grinding and polishing it on both sides. The float process has just one mechanized procedure.

Liquid glass pours out of the furnace on to giant rollers and then floats onto a bed of molten tin, producing a large expanse of glass with an immaculate fire-polished surface. Made in continuous ribbons, the glass passes over more rollers to a lehr and is annealed. Huge sheets can be made from ⅛in. to 1in. (4mm–25mm) thick, and toughened through repeated cooling and heating. The same method can be applied to produce patterned sheets by using textured rollers to impress decorative details onto the surface of the glass. A range of pot metal and flashed glass sheets that imitate the traditionally blown antique glass are produced specifically for making stained glass.

Clear float glass, also known as soda or window glass, is used by architectural glass artists who are able to transform this everyday material into an exciting medium. Its flawless surface makes it easy to cut and perfect for creating textural contrasts through sandblasting and acid etching. Grooves can be cut in the glass, or beveled angles made through repeated grinding and polishing. It provides an ideal canvas for enamels and lusters, and in the heat of the kiln sheets of float glass can be fused in layers or slumped and bent under their own weight or broken into small fragments and cast into almost any form.

Dichroic glass, coated with a thin layer of a metallic oxide, is a relatively new type of float glass. It is both transparent and reflective, which perhaps explains its growing appeal with architectural artists. As light passes through dichroic glass it is filtered to a single color, but as light is reflected from the surface of the glass a complementary color is revealed. Depending on the angle of reflection, varying tones of these two opposing hues are produced.

Float glass is produced by a mechanized process that has replaced the separate and labor-intensive stages of making flat glass. Here, a huge sheet of float glass is being cut to size using a diamond saw. (left).

Multicolored frit and shards are
picked up on the blowing iron
with a bubble of molten glass to
be reheated, blown, and spun
into a colorful roundel of crown
glass (*right and detail below*).

RODS, TUBES; SHARDS, AND FRIT

Kiln techniques such as fusing and casting make use of the wide variety
of glass available, including rods, tubes, shards, frit, and cullet. In the
kiln, these different forms of glass can be sandwiched between layers of
window glass and fused together or used for casting with molds. Whole
sheets of glass can be made in this way, either fused together from fine
powders, or cast out of glass granules called frit or chunks of glass
known as cullet.

Rods are a versatile form of glass, widely used in ancient kiln-
glass techniques. They are made by drawing molten glass directly out of
the furnace into different-size threads of color. Tubing is made in a similar
way by drawing out a thread of molten glass while a stream of air is
blown through the middle of it. Rods and tubes can be lamp-worked
using a burner to soften the glass and bend it into curves and twists.
Alternatively, different colored rods can be bunched and melted together,
cut into decorative slices, then later fused again to form shallow bowls,
plates, or dishes.

Shards of glass, used in both casting and fusing, are made from
large bubbles of colored glass blown out like a balloon and then
shattered into the thinnest fragments. Another material for kiln-worked
glass is frit, a clear or colored glass mechanically crushed from larger
ingots into small irregular granules. The pieces of glass are then sieved
through a series of gradating meshes, separating them into sizes ranging
from considerable grains to fine powders.

All of these types of glass can also be used to color crown
glass or other blown forms. The initial bubble of molten glass is rolled on
a bed of colored frit, powders, rods, or shards, which adhere to its hot
surface. It is then reheated into a single blob that, when blown and spun
out into a disk, forms a complex spiral pattern of colored streaks.

LEAD

A pliable material, easy to cut and solder, and particularly well suited to forming tight curves and intricate designs, lead has, since the eleventh century, played an essential part in the manufacture of traditional stained glass. Grooved lengths of rod known as cames (or calmes) are wrapped around the edge of the glass and soldered to hold the glass in place. Originally lead cames were made by pouring molten lead into a rectangular wooden box in which reeds or straight twigs were arranged in neat lines over a layer of sand. The heat of the lead, caused the reeds to burn away, leaving hollow tubes in a sheet of lead, which was then cut into strips and used for glazing. Nowadays, more modern methods are employed, so lead is either factory molded or extruded.

Attitudes to the use of lead have changed throughout the history of stained glass. In medieval glass, lead was primarily a structural material that was integrated into the design to support the glass. Later, after the Renaissance and as the style of glassmaking changed, lead was regarded as a necessary evil that artists tried to camouflage within the design. In the twentieth century, the tendency has been for artists to use lead in a more overt and expressive way. By sculpting and manipulating the lead into free-flowing lines of patterns or, conversely, using it in a rigid geometric way, artists are now going beyond its purely structural benefits and incorporating it as an important part of the design in its own right.

Recently, metals other than lead have become increasingly popular, particularly for artists producing large-scale work. Zinc, brass, and copper, for example, have greater structural strength and can therefore support larger pieces of glass but they are harder to manipulate. Artists are continually experimenting with innovative ways of supporting flat glass. Clasps or shackles can be used to hold glass in place on steel cables that are fastened under tension; the glass can be drilled and bolted onto a wood or metal frame; or it can be fixed with modern glues, which have opened up many new possibilities for working with the material.

Lead, which is used to hold glass in place, has played an important part in the creation of stained glass for centuries. Here, a piece of stretched lead is being opened with a latheskin in preparation for inserting the glass (left).

A variety of specialist tools is used in glassmaking. Here, a selection of these tools is used to restore a glass panel (far right and detail right).

TRADITIONAL TOOLS

An assortment of simple tools is needed to make a leaded window. First the glass has to be cut, usually with a steel or tungsten carbide wheel cutter. The line of the cut is marked on the glass with a Chinagraph pencil, and the cutter is guided along it with enough downward pressure to score the glass and create a fracture. To facilitate the movement of the cutting wheel, especially when cutting complicated curves and sharp corners, a small amount of lubricating oil can be painted onto the glass.

Once the surface cut has been made, the glass is snapped along the line of the cut either by hand or with breaking pliers that exert pressure on the cut line, helping to keep the fracture clean. Special grozing pliers—with one jaw curved and one flat—are used to snap off any unwanted fragments of glass that have failed to break off along the cut line. Any rough edges are smoothed with a Carborundum file or sickle stone.

After cutting, the glass is ready to be decorated. Enamels or silver stain can be applied with different types of brushes, many of them specifically manufactured for stained-glass work. For example, a tracing brush is a thin, long-haired brush, made from sable, ox, or camel hair, and is ideally suited to painting outlines. A broad badger brush is the best tool for traditional shading—a technique that is known as matting. After decoration, the glass must be fired in a kiln at various temperatures up to 1382°F (750°C), depending on the type of enamel or stain that has been applied.

A lead stretcher, oyster knife, grozing pliers, copper ties, latheskin, brushes, and gas soldering iron with tallow are some of the tools that are used to create a stained-glass window (far left and detail left).

For leading a stained-glass panel, a special vice is needed to stretch the lengths of lead to remove any kinks or wrinkles. The stretched lead is cut to different sizes and at different angles with a heavy-handled flat-bladed lead knife. A stopping, or oyster, knife and a smooth wooden tool called a latheskin are then used to open and straighten the flanges of the lead in preparation for inserting the glass. Before the lead pieces are soldered together, using a gas or electric soldering iron, all the joins are abraded and cleaned with a small wire brush. When both sides of the panel have been soldered, a strengthening cement, applied with a stiff-bristled scrubbing brush, is worked into the crevices between the glass and lead cames.

For additional techniques, other specialist equipment may be needed, such as diamond saws and drills to slice the glass and make holes to bolt panels on to a framework, or thread with wire to suspend the glass. Lathes with various grinding, cutting, and polishing wheels are used for beveling, shaping, or decorative cutting, and a sandblaster is used to create frosting and textural contrast on the surface of the glass. A water-fed flexible drive is invaluable for etching and carving into the glass. This versatile hand-held tool consists of rotating diamond heads or tiny polishing wheels that can be changed to lightly engrave the glass, carve deeply into it, or vigorously polish it.

TECHNIQUES

A diverse range of techniques is
available to artists working with
glass. This section looks at these
techniques, some of which have
been used for centuries, and others
which have been discovered more
recently as artists explore new
opportunities to create ever more
inspiring and challenging pieces
of work.

Glass being
selected and cut
for a traditional
panel

TRADITIONAL GLAZING

Techniques for traditional stained glass were described by the monk Theophilus, around A.D. 1100:

> If you want to assemble simple windows, first mark out the dimensions of their length and breadth on a wooden board, then draw scroll work or anything else that pleases you, and select colors that are to be put in. Cut the glass and fit the pieces together with a grozing iron. Enclose them with lead calms, and solder on both sides. Surround it with a wooden frame strengthened with nails and set it up in the place where you wish.

These methods are still largely used today, little has changed in 900 years. The first steps in making stained glass are to survey the site and take measurements. Once a design has been decided on, a full-scale drawing, or cartoon, must be prepared. The cartoon, which can either be done by hand or photographically enlarged from sketches, is the blueprint for the work. It includes all the different sizes, shapes, colors, and types of glass and any painted or other decorative details, along with the dimensions of the lead. The individual pieces of glass are cut to fit the cartoon, like a jigsaw, before being stuck to a sheet of clear glass using wax or Plasticine. This gives a preview of the panel, showing the separate colors and textures of glass working together as a whole. At this stage, each section of glass can be worked on with additional techniques such as sandblasting or enameling to add depth and texture to the piece. The finished glass is then transferred piecemeal into a lattice of lead.

Once a design for a stained-glass window has been decided, the required pieces of glass are cut to shape *(left)*. The finished design can be a mixture of colors and shapes. Here, antique glass is leaded with lenses and a blown roundel of clear glass (James B. Furman, *City Health Club Window*, detail) *(below)*.

Once the glass and lead
are in place, the panel is
cemented to hold everything
together. To help the cement set,
the panel is repeatedly coated,
cleaned off and then coated
again with a chalky powder—a
process called whitening *(right)*.

Before use, the lead cames are prepared by stretching and cutting them
to size. The flanges along the lead cames are opened using an oyster
knife or latheskin to enable the glass to be slotted between them. The
cames are then bent and shaped around the pieces of glass, which are
inserted piece by piece and held in place on a sturdy leading bench
within a framework of battens and nails.

When all the glass is in place the lead is soldered at every
junction alternately on both sides of the panel. It is held in place with
a sticky linseed-oil-based cement, which is forced into all the crevices
between the glass and the lead using a thick-bristled brush. The
cemented panel is coated with a chalky powder to aid setting, after
which the excess cement is cleaned off with a sharp tool. When
hardened, the cement secures the glass to the lead and ensures the
window is sturdy and waterproof.

To support the finished panel in the window frame, strategically
placed copper wires or bands of lead or zinc are soldered onto the
lead to act as fasteners for what are known as saddle bars. These are
a structural network of steel bars set into the masonry of a window to
support the panel and prevent larger leaded panels from buckling under
their own weight. Saddle bars, if needed, are bent and shaped to fit
along the contours of the lead lines to avoid spoiling the design. Fixed
division bars, in the form of a structural grid, are an alternative way of
supporting and strengthening a window. With this method, several
smaller panels, each comprising part of the design, are constructed
separately and then individually mounted between the metal bars.

PAINTING AND STAINING

Part of the appeal of glass as an artistic medium is that it can be painted or stained to create an almost infinite number of tones, ranging from completely opaque to virtually transparent.

The two main types of glass paints are enamels and metallic lusters, both of which are applied in similar ways. They can be painted on evenly with a brush or stippled, sponged, blotted, ragged, or sieved, or even screen-printed or airbrushed. The glass is then fired in the kiln to temperatures over 932°F (500°C) to fix the paints.

Enamels are principally finely ground powdered glass with one or more metal oxides added as coloring agents, along with a flux to aid the melting of the glass powder in the kiln. For easy application, the powdered enamels are mixed with water and a binder, such as gum arabic. Depending on the types of enamels, when fired they appear either watery and translucent or opaque and impenetrable, forming blocks of striking color. For additional texture, thin copper wire or shards and granules of glass can be added to the enamel, which, when fired, acts like a glue sticking to the main body of glass.

Tracing and matting are two traditional types of glass painting in which an opaque dark-red to brownish-black iron oxide enamel is used, specifically for bold outlines and shading. The enamel is applied to the glass with a badger- or camel-hair brush and, while it is still wet, certain areas are wiped out, creating highlights, or partially removed with brushes and cloths to produce a gradation of tone. Alternatively, the enamel can be left to dry and then partly scratched off using an assortment of sharp tools.

Painting or staining glass enables artists to create some beautifully vivid results. Various brushes can be used for a diversity of effects *(left)*. Here, vitreous paints, enamels, and silver stain have been painted onto acid-etched antique glass. (Linda Litchman, *Jazz Tapestry*, detail) *(above)*.

Using enamels or lusters, glass artists can create the most intricate of designs. Here, the glass painter is taking out the matt with a short bristle brush to produce a feathery effect (right).

Lusters are a metallic compound that, in the kiln, deposits a small amount of metal on the surface of the glass, producing vibrant iridescent colors. Since lusters all fire at the same temperature, they can be layered and mixed more readily than enamels, which require different temperatures depending on the pigment or oxide used.

Silver staining was first developed in the early fourteenth century and is how the term "stained glass" was coined. A silver nitrate paste is applied to the surface of the glass, which is then heated to around 1202°F (650°C) in the kiln. During firing, silver ions migrate into the body of the glass, imparting varying shades of yellow, from the faintest hint of lemon to a dark golden amber. This procedure produces a permanent stain, quite different from enameling, which creates surface color that could eventually wear away. The same piece of glass can be painted with enamels as well as stained—although this is usually on the opposite side of the glass.

As an alternative to kiln-fired paints, a selection of oil- or resin-based paints can be airbrushed or painted straight onto the glass and set without firing. They are more fragile than enameled colors, but are easy to use and come in a range of intermixable transparent hues.

Despite the wide range of specialist stained-glass paints available, some artists find that experimenting with other materials can yield more unusual and exciting results. Artists have tried using ceramic glazes mixed with metal powders, car body paints, oil paints, or even pencil fixed with a lacquer or varnish among other things.

SANDBLASTING

Spraying glass with various grades of sand or grit in a jet of air—a process known as sandblasting—gives the surface a translucent frosted appearance. Heavy sandblasting can form deep sculpted contours in the glass, affording a strong three-dimensional impression when the glass is viewed from the other side. Lighter blasting on the immaculate surface of float glass offers a tremendous contrast from clear to translucent, creating varying tones, depths, and textures as the light diffuses from the mat surface. Sandblasting can also be used to cut glass when an irregular edge or a complicated shape is required. After sandblasting, the glass can be fired or treated with acid to give a polished effect, rendering the now-contoured glass smooth and transparent once more.

To transfer the design onto the glass, a stencil is used. The stencil is made out of anything that will withstand the force of the sand being fired at it under great pressure. The most common material is self-adhesive vinyl sheeting, which is stuck to the glass and then cut away in parts to reveal the pattern of bare glass ready for blasting. The cutting can be done by hand or by computer-controlled cutters for greater precision and more intricate designs. Glue and wax can also be painted, poured, or dripped onto the glass, and built up in layers to withstand heavier blasting. Experimenting with other materials—natural and synthetic—such as leaves and branches, netting, wire mesh, or even delicate pieces of lace, for more subtle blasting can produce some beautiful and interesting effects.

Flashed glass lends itself particularly well to sandblasting because when the colored surface glass is eroded, the contrasting base glass beneath is revealed. Sandblasting can also be combined with other techniques such as acid etching or painting with enamels, either before or after blasting, adding color to depth and texture.

The finishing touches are made to a hand-cut vinyl stencil. This will be sandblasted to produce a pattern on the glass (left). Sandblasting with a coarse grit can give glass a beautiful textured and grainy appearance (below).

These glass screens have been acid etched to produce intricate maps with bold images that mirror the terrazzo floors surrounding the building (Martin Donlin, Sunderland City Library and Arts Centre, detail) *(above)*. This design has undergone several acid treatments to cut through layers of flashed antique glass (John K. Clark, *Pibroch Windows*, detail) *(right)*.

ACID ETCHING

As its name suggests, acid etching involves dissolving the top surface of glass with strong acid. Acid etching, like sandblasting, is well suited to flashed glass because the acid corrodes the top layer of colored glass, revealing a different layer beneath. The depth of erosion can be skillfully controlled, creating subtle variations in tone, by only partially removing the surface color in different stages. Before etching, the glass is masked off with a "resist," to protect the area that is not going to be exposed to the acid. Wax, which can be expressively painted onto the glass, and vinyl stencils—either hand- or machine- cut—are both commonly used. For deeper etching, bitumen or Brunswick black are the most durable and effective. With the resist in place, the glass is immersed in a bath of hydrofluoric acid and left for the required time, anything from a few minutes to twenty-four hours. Alternatively, a small wall of fat, such as lard and beeswax, can be built up around the edges of the glass to retain the acid as it is poured onto the glass.

Acid etching on float glass produces a similar effect to the frosting achieved with sandblasting, but with a smoother, softer, more controlled finish. A variety of results can be obtained depending on the way in which the resist is applied and the length of exposure: very fine detailed work can be accomplished when resists are screen-printed on and only the thinnest surface layer is removed, or deeper corrosive effects can be achieved if the masked glass is left in the acid for several hours. Acid-etched glass can also be painted or stained, and when used with a double flash the combination of colored layers can create endless shades.

FUSING

Several separate pieces of glass can be combined through heat into a single piece in a process known as fusing. Glass fragments are either overlaid or positioned side by side in a kiln and heated to 1292–1472°F (700–800°C). At this temperature the surface of the glass softens and flows, causing the pieces of glass to unite and bond permanently.

This ancient technique was first developed in the Bronze Age, when it was used to make mosaic glass vessels. Colored glass rods were carefully bunched together so that when fused and cut into transverse slices, a multicolored cross section of pattern was revealed. The slices of colored glass were then closely arranged in a two-piece mold. The first piece was the shape of the desired plate, bowl, or beaker, and the other one, slightly smaller, fitted inside it, with the slices of glass sandwiched between them. When placed in a kiln and fired, the glass re-fused, taking on the form of the mold. After cooling the mold was removed and the vessel was polished using lathes and abrasive powders.

Today, fusing is increasingly popular with architectural glass artists, particularly because it is extremely versatile and can be adapted to suit individual ways of working. Flat pieces of colored glass can be fused onto a sheet of clear—or colored—base glass, allowing artists to design large panels with all the richness of traditional stained glass but without having to use lead lines. Sheet glass can also be fused in multiple layers to create relief forms that are several inches deep. The key to perfect fusing is compatibility of materials—it is essential that all the individual components expand and contract at a similar rate when heated or cooled, otherwise the stress created in the glass is likely to cause it to break.

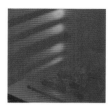

When making this glass tile (designed by Jon Lewis), triangular pieces of 1in. (25mm) float glass were first coated with a green powdered enamel, and then randomly positioned on to a sheet of ½in.(10mm) float glass, ready for fusing (*left*). The glass is placed in a kiln and slowly heated until red hot—approximately 1472°F (800°C) at which point the glass softens and the separate pieces join together (*above*).

The effect of heating can be seen in the finished piece, where the triangle pieces of glass have sagged outwards, losing their sharp edges (*left*).

Colored frit can be fused with float glass by sprinkling it, in the desired pattern, onto sheets of heat-resistant ceramic fiber paper. This is overlaid with a sheet of window glass and placed in the kiln where the two fuse, producing a colorful and textural effect. Frit, together with rods, shards, and enamels, can also be sandwiched between sheets of clear glass before firing. A wide range of other substances can produce interesting effects when fused between layers of glass: copper wire, metal foils, threads, and powders create unpredictable patterns of color when they oxidize in the kiln; washing soda produces decorative bubbles trapped in the glass; and natural materials such as seeds or bones leave delicate traces of pattern when they carbonize within fused glass.

Fusing glass can be a very immediate experience, full of possibilities. The process gets really exciting when a sheet of molten glass—the blank canvas—is taken out of the kiln and is only hot enough to be worked on by the artist for a limited amount of time. Glass powders and granules in a multitude of colors can be scattered onto the molten surface, instantly melting and fusing with it. Threadlike rods of glass form irregular lines as they merge with it, and shards fuse with the glass in abstract shapes. Every now and then the piece is reheated with a powerful blowtorch to delay the moment when the glass has to be returned to the kiln. If the glass is allowed to become too cool, the resulting stresses will cause it to crack. Once finished, the newly colored and textured glass is placed back in the kiln to continue the fusing process and to anneal.

Slumping is used to create a diverse range of architectural designs in glass. Here, float glass is slumped into a mold for washbasins (designed by Jeff Bell) *(left)*. Casting is also a popular technique; here, colored bricks have been cast in a sand mold (Daniela Granzin, *Colored Glassbricks*, detail) *(above)*.

SLUMPING AND CASTING

Architectural glass artists use the kiln technique of slumping to create curves, texture, and low-relief forms out of sheet glass. The glass is placed over a former, into a mold, or even suspended from wires, to assist in shaping the glass as it is heated in the kiln. As the kiln temperature rises, the glass softens and eventually sags under its own weight, taking on the form of the mold.

There are several ways of adapting this technique to suit the demands of the design. Slumping molds can be made of metal or cast from wet plaster, mixed with special heat-resistant ceramic fibers and silica. By casting the mold onto a textured surface, such as a bed of leaves, a delicate imprint is left on the surface of the mold, which will later be transferred to the glass. Another way to produce markings that will appear on the glass is to carve or scratch the surface of the cast once it has hardened. The mold can also be painted with enamels, which will be picked up by the slumping glass as it relaxes in the heat of the kiln. This technique is particularly useful for highlighting specific areas in color. Alternatively, for greater texture and more relief, models made out of clay, wax, cardboard, string, fabric, or any other appropriate media can be cast out of heat-resistant materials into a shallow open mold for the slumping glass.

Casting is a very versatile technique that allows artists to manipulate glass into almost any shape. There are endless possibilities, including open casting molds that are filled with glass and then fired in the kiln *(right)*. Once fired, the glass is broken from around the glass mold (Jeff Bell, *stair tread*) *(far right)*.

Casting is another method that uses a mold to shape glass, but in this case sheets of glass are not essential. Casting glass takes place at a much higher temperature than slumping or fusing, which means that the viscosity of the glass is very different. At around 1652°F (900°C) the glass is in liquid form and can flow into almost any shape. In the field of architectural glass, patterned and textured sheets can be cast from glass cullet, ingots or slabs of glass. The mold itself can be decorated, scattered with colored frit, metal oxides, copper wire, rods, or enamels, which are incorporated into the liquid glass in order to enrich the quality of the finished piece.

The *pâte de verre* (French for "paste of glass") casting technique was developed in France in the late nineteenth century as a result of attempts to re-create ancient Egyptian methods of glassmaking. Glass grains or powders are packed tightly into a mold, which is then fired, fusing the grains of glass together. This can give the glass surface a characteristic textured and granular appearance. One of the advantages of this technique over casting with larger ingots, cullet or slabs of glass is that it enables the artist to determine the position of color and detail precisely. Although most commonly known for its use in making decorative vessels and small sculpture, *pâte de verre* has also been used for flat pieces such as glass cases, screens, and church windows.

CUTTING, GRINDING, AND POLISHING

Glass can be cut, ground, and polished to give shape, smoothness, or texture. The techniques involved in these processes actually predate the Romans and were initially used on early cast glass in the final stages of production with polishing wheels on primitive lathes. Today's techniques are not dissimilar; cutting lathes with wheels of different shapes and sizes, polishing machines, and rotary hand-held tools are among the variety of mechanized equipment used in conjunction with varying grades of pumice or grit mixed with water. Stone, diamond, and cork wheels grind and roughen the glass, shaping it by abrading and wearing away its surface. After grinding, the softer felt and rag wheels are used for smoothing the glass, creating flawless polished areas. Homemade fiberboard wheels are also effective and, with the right abrasive powders, can be used for both cutting and polishing. Brilliant cutting uses a hard wheel with a special V-shaped edge to create sharp cuts in the glass, whereas beveling—generally done on a horizontal grinding wheel—makes polished angles on the edges of the glass by grinding and polishing. Concave circles can also be ground into the surface of the glass and when highly polished act like clear windows amid a sandblasted or flashed colored surface.

Since polishing glass by hand is so time consuming and laborious, computer-controlled machines have been developed to perform the task. The drawback is that the finished glass can lack transparency and may have to be completed by hand, using diamond files and abrasive papers.

The various wheels on the lathe can be used to grind and polish glass into the desired shape and texture (*left*). In this piece of work, grooves have been cut into the glass using a diamond saw (Alexander Beleschenko, *The Garden Quadrangle*, St. John's College, Oxford, detail) (*below*).

GLASS BONDING

Until the invention of the *dalle de verre* (French for "slabs of glass") technique, lead was a prerequisite for making stained glass. This alternative to lead was first developed in France in the 1930s and became popular throughout Europe and America after World War II.

The process involves embedding colored slabs of glass, approximately 1in. (3cm) thick, in an epoxy resin or cement. The slabs are first roughly cut with a traditional glass cutter and then finished—and often faceted—by placing them on an anvil and chipping away at them with a sharp-edged hammer. Windows are made by laying a pattern of cut slabs into a shallow wooden tray, with enough space between each slab for the epoxy resin or cement to be poured around them; once set, the resin provides a chunky support for the glass.

Although the *dalle de verre* method is rarely used today, this early use of epoxy as an alternative to lead was the forerunner of the current use of synthetic adhesives in contemporary architectural glass. Many subsequent experiments with adhesives were short-lived because differences in the degree of thermal expansion between different types of glass and the adhesive eventually led to cracking and failure of the bond when subjected to day-to-day temperature changes.

Modern specialist glass glues, which are often cured by ultraviolet light, have flexible qualities allowing for slight movement in the glass. This gives artists the freedom to construct large panels of richly colored glass without the use of lead. Different types of glass can be layered on top of each other with no limitations as to the size of the kiln or their compatibility when heated. Antique glass can be laminated onto or sandwiched between huge sheets of float glass, creating a vivid stained-glass effect with no obvious structural lines. Chunks of colored glass, small beveled pieces or sections of cut and highly polished glass can be glued to already etched or sandblasted float glass, forming detailed areas of color and texture. Using modern glues, whole sheets of glass can be made up of hundreds—or even thousands—of tiny pieces stuck together to form one shimmering and glittering window.

Modern glues have increased the flexibility of working with glass, allowing artists to work with much larger panels and combine different types of glass. Here, antique glass is being laminated onto float glass (designed by Susan Ting) *(right)*, and glass disks, lenses, and pieces of dichronic glass are bonded to laminated and sandblasted float glass (Laura Johnston, *Curved Light Screen*, detail) *(below)*.

GALLERY

The use of stained or architectural

glass has become increasingly

popular as an artistic medium

during the twentieth century.

In this section, a collection of work

from the growing number of

contemporary artists working with

glass is showcased, highlighting

the versatile and exciting nature of

this medium.

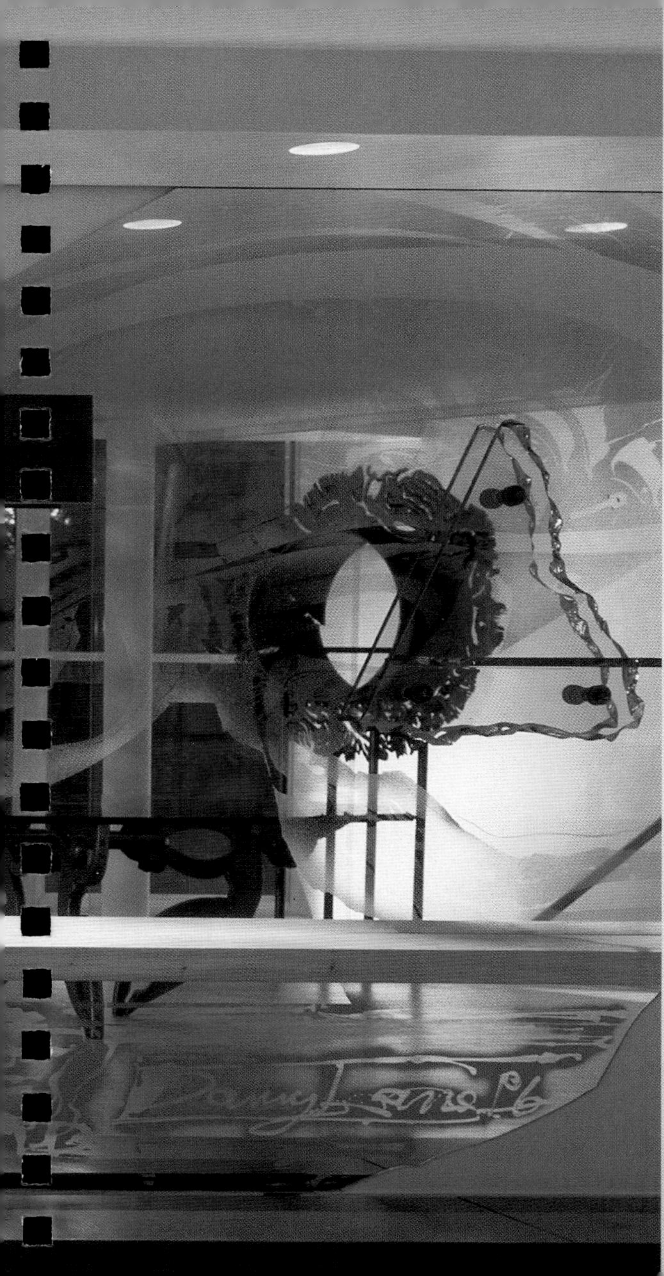

Dear David
3D glass screen,
commissioned for a
private residence.
Danny Lane

GLASS

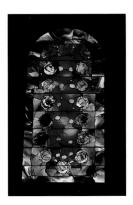

MARK ANGUS

Daily Bread, the vibrant window by the British artist Mark Angus, can be seen in the north aisle of Durham Cathedral. The exquisite colors are due to the distinctive, predominantly streaky, mouth-blown glass selected by the artist. The expressive use of lead connects the individual pieces with fine erratic lines, adding movement and presence to the window. Clearly reminiscent of scenes of the *Last Supper*, the piece is based on the theme of physical and spiritual food. Angus works principally with glass and lead, although some of his work includes staining, etching, and painting techniques as well as photographic silk-screen printing onto the glass.

Daily Bread

North aisle window, commissioned by Durham Cathedral, England

Mark Angus 1983

TRANSFORMATION, IN THIS CASE PHYSICAL FOOD INTO SPIRITUAL FOOD, IS AT THE HEART OF WORKING WITH COLORED LIGHT, JUST AS IT IS AT THE HEART OF THE SACRAMENT. A VARIED GROUP OF PEOPLE SIT TOGETHER AROUND A TABLE SHARING FOOD AND DRINK, LINKING HEAVEN AND EARTH ACROSS TIME. WHEN WORKING WITHIN THE CHURCH THESE MARVELOUS MOMENTS OF CREATIVITY ARE FOUND.

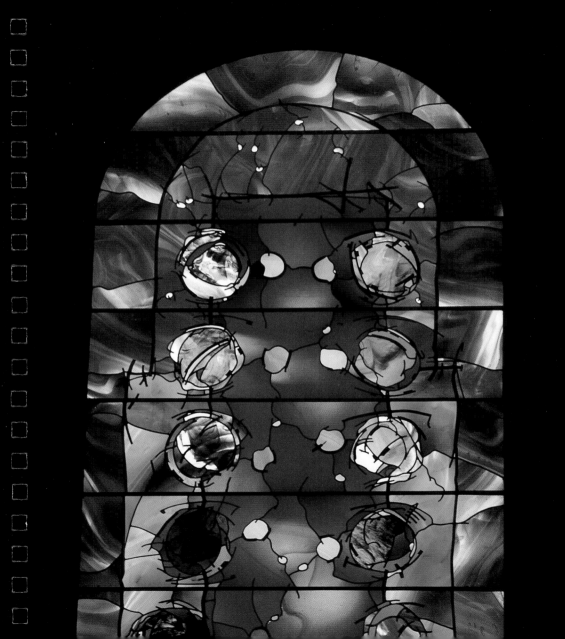

ALEXANDER BELESCHENKO

After training in fine art, Beleschenko spent two years in Italy, which inspired him to start working in stained glass. He now focuses on glass art in architecture. Beleschenko's five glass screens stand in a new building at St. John's College, Oxford, and are made up of about 60,000 separate pieces of glass weighing over 3.5 tons. In response to the surrounding cavelike architecture of this part of the building known as The Underworld, the screens suggest running water and glistening rocks in a subterranean realm. The greater part of the work is made from crystal-clear ⅜in. (10mm) float glass, accurately cut into squares and framed within a matrix of clear and colored glass strips. Each square has been individually worked on, using specially adapted machine tools to score, chip, and roughen the glass, scattering the light in a glinting dance across its surface.

Glass screens for atrium

St. John's College, Oxford, England
663 sq. ft. (62m²)
Alexander Beleschenko 1993

'IN SOME AREAS A WEB OF LIGHT IS TRAPPED IN THE SPARKLE OF THE EDGE DETAILS, WHEREAS OTHER AREAS HOLD THE GLOW OF A WHITE LIGHT IN THE SAWN DETAILS. THIS PLAY OF LIGHT TRAPPED IN THE MATRIX IS SEEN AS THE UNDERLYING PRINCIPLE IN MY APPROACH TO WORKING THE GLASS.'

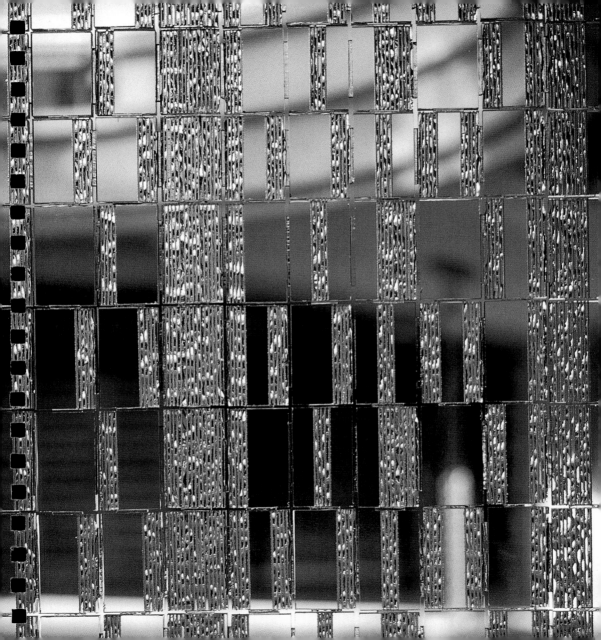

JEFF BELL

Jeff Bell designs, manufactures, and installs architectural elements in cast and slumped glass, ranging from large-scale sculptural installations to simple bowls, furniture, decorative screens, and stair treads. His relationship with the glass is an ambivalent one— he is fascinated and challenged by the diversity of the material and its constant changes in response to temperature, but also frustrated by its untouchable and unpredictable characteristics in the kiln. Although he has some degree of control over the glass, through the use of molds and careful regulation of the kiln temperature, no matter how scientific his methods, the glass always emerges from the kiln with its own "life."

Now and Zen

Water feature for Now and Zen restaurant, London, England. 24 water-filled, kiln-formed bowls spiral down through three floors

Jeff Bell 1991

EACH COMMISSION COMES WITH ITS OWN SET OF TECHNICAL PROBLEMS WHICH HAVE TO BE RESOLVED, CREATING FURTHER POSSIBILITIES FOR THE MATERIAL AND OPPORTUNITIES IN WORKING WITH GLASS.

PHILIPPA BEVERIDGE

After four years working as
a landscape architect in London,
Philippa Beveridge moved to
Barcelona to study glass. This
move was prompted by her first
visit to the city as a graduate,
when she became interested in
stained glass and mosaics, initially
as a possible application within her
field. She has since studied mosaic
and stained glass for three years
at the Massana School of Art, with
further studies in advanced glass
techniques at the Fundancio Center
Del Vidre in Barcelona. Influences
from her first career come through
in her glass work as she draws
on aspects from nature and
architecture. In the work *Light
Wall*, a collage of copper, silver,
and gold foils has been placed
between layers of float glass,
positioned in the kiln, and
simultaneously fused and slumped.

Pared de Luz (Light Wall)
Fused and slumped glass with metal
inclusions, Barcelona, Spain
Philippa Beveridge 1998

LIGHT WALL IS INSPIRED BY THE WAY IN WHICH THE
FACADES OF BUILDINGS REVEAL THE PASSING OF TIME
AND, IN DOING SO, THE PASSING OF LIFE. THE TEXTURES
AND COLORS WERE TAKEN FROM A PHOTOMONTAGE OF
DECAYING WALLS AND THE RELIEF IN THE GLASS WAS
CREATED USING BUILDING DEBRIS.

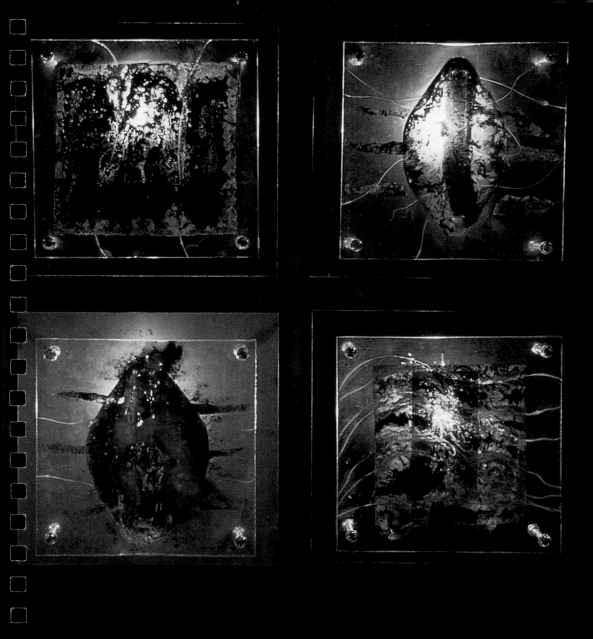

ED CARPENTER

The 57ft. (17.4m) high steel and glass screen standing behind the altar at St. Mark's Cathedral in Seattle is one of the many large-scale public works designed by the glass artist Ed Carpenter. After being introduced to architecture at an early age, Carpenter went on to study architectural glass in England and Germany, and subsequently has completed more than 50 large-scale collaborative glass commissions. The glass work at St. Mark's is a free-standing structure, supporting a rose 28ft. (8.5m) in diameter near the top. Made with 184 pieces of plate glass fixed into a steel framework, the piece is illuminated by the daylight that comes pouring in from the circular window behind. Around the circumference of the rose, dichroic glass petals create an array of colored light, reflecting a constantly changing spectrum of colors onto the cathedral's walls.

Altar screen and rose

St. Mark's Episcopal Cathedral, Seattle, Washington

Ed Carpenter in collaboration with architect Jim Olson 1997

REPRESENTING HARMONY AND DIVINE LOGIC AND RICH WITH SYMBOLISM, THE ROSE IS REMINISCENT OF THE ANCIENT ROSE WINDOWS IN THE GOTHIC CATHEDRALS OF EUROPE. IT IS THE ALMOST UNIVERSAL SYMBOL OF TIME AND ETERNITY.

One of the most respected glass artists working in America today, Dale Chihuly is best known for his large and colorful, handblown glass forms which, in more recent commissions, he has attached to walls or windows to make vast collage-like sculptures. All his work has an organic quality and his "Persians", as he has christened the large glass roundels in this piece, look like butterflies or flowers. The Monarch Window provides just one of Chihuly's sculptural centerpieces created for the renovated, Beaux Arts, Union Station building at Tacoma in Washington. To create his assemblages, the artist works with teams of glassblowers—as many as half-a-dozen artisans working together, each with his or her specific task. Chihuly founded the Pilchuck Glass School in 1971.

Monarch Window

Commissioned for the Tacoma Union
Station Building, Tacoma, Washington
40ft. by 22ft. by 3ft. (12m by 6.7m
by 0.9m)

Dale Chihuly 1994

THE UNION STATION IS A TOUGH SPACE . . . IT'S LIKE
DECORATING THE INSIDE OF A CATHEDRAL. YOU HAVE TO
BE VERY SENSITIVE TO WHAT THIS PLACE IS.

JOHN K. CLARK

The Scottish artist John Clark works principally as a glass artist. Before designing a piece, detailed research into the subject matter and the requirements of the commission are conducted. This is an essential part of the designing process, and only when complete are the composition elements, imagery, and symbolism considered. The incredible detail and masterly control of etching, painting, and silver staining are the most identifiable characteristics of Clark's work. He considers these traditional techniques as "the core of the art form that is called stained glass, and by working with them something truly original can be created."

The Battle at Waternish

One of the three Pibroch Windows commissioned by the Piping Centre, Glasgow, Scotland (right). Detail of the window in progress (far right).

John Clark 1996

AN ASPECT OF MY WORK THAT I FIND INTRIGUING AT PRESENT IS THE COMBINATION OF TEXTS AND SYMBOLS IN A SINGLE INTERRELATED IMAGE. IT IS ALMOST A CUBIST CONCEPT. THERE IS NO BACKGROUND OR FOREGROUND, JUST A FORM OF SPACE. THIS CREATES A MULTILAYERED IMAGE THAT HAS MANY SIMILARITIES TO MUSIC, AND INDEED IT WAS THIS APPROACH I USED FOR THE PIBROCH WINDOWS, WHICH ARE AN ATTEMPTED VISUALIZATION OF SCOTTISH BAGPIPE MUSIC.

ELIZABETH DEVEREAUX

With her strong academic and practical background, artist Elizabeth Devereaux is uniquely qualified in the field of architectural glass. Her degree in painting and drawing was followed by postgraduate work in industrial design, the craft of stained glass, and religious art and architecture. She has brought together her artistic skill and her knowledge of materials, architecture, and liturgy to create works of art mainly in churches, but also in public, commercial, and residential buildings. Devereaux almost always uses mouth-blown glass, which is often blown to her specifications, perhaps flashed with multiple layers of color and etched to create subtle gradations of tone, or painted and kiln fired.

Hosanna in the Highest

Choir window, one of 18 windows at St. Elizabeth Ann Seton Catholic Church, Rowland Heights, California
3¼ft. by 6½ft. (1m by 2m)

Elizabeth Devereaux 1990

"WHETHER THE SITE PROVIDES A LUXURIANT LANDSCAPE OR AN UNSIGHTLY VIEW; WHETHER IT IS A RESTORATION OF A NATIONAL LANDMARK OR A SIMPLE AND SLEEK ARCHITECTURAL STATEMENT, THE PROCESS IS THE SAME. THOUGHTFUL, APPROPRIATE, AND CREATIVE DESIGNS ARE PROPOSED AND COLLABORATIVE SOLUTIONS ARE AGREED. UPON WHICH FULLY INTEGRATE THE GLASS INTO ITS SETTING."

MARTIN DONLIN

Continuing the long tradition of storytelling in glass, Martin Donlin uses classical figures and abstract representational imagery to play a variety of roles in his work. Image, form, and text may relate to the physical characteristics of the area, refer to the historical heritage, or act as a marker and identity for the site. The free-standing canopy, located in a main street in Middlesbrough, a steel-making center in the north of England, was the result of a national competition to create a meeting place for local people. Toughened float glass suspended from cables is enameled with early maps of the area and the image of the ancient fire god Vulcan at his forge, alluding to the city's industrial heritage.

Free-standing canopy

Linthorpe Road, Middlesbrough, England
Glass and steel: glass 33ft. by 23ft.
(10m by 7m); steel 33ft. (10m) high

Martin Donlin 1997

'MY WORK CAN PLAY DIFFERENT ROLES THROUGHT THE USE OF IMAGE, FORM, AND TEXT. IT CAN RELATE TO THE PHYSICAL CHARACTERISTICS OF A SITE. IT CAN REFER TO THE HISTORICAL HERITAGE AND MEANING OF A SITE, OR IT CAN ACT AS A MARKER ESTABLISHING AN IDENTITY OF A SITE CREATING A SENSE OF PLACE.'

JAMES B. FURMAN

For more than 20 years, James Furman has designed and fabricated contemporary leaded-glass works, using antique, crown and float glass, for private residences and public buildings. Furman's vast windows, in the main entrance to St. Andrew's in Gibbsboro, New Jersey, are inspired by the theme of goodness and the beauty of creation. The concept of goodness is expressed by the use of much clear glass, which allows an abundance of unrestricted light into the building, giving a feeling of openness and harmony. The beauty of creation is shown "as a bringing together of heaven and earth" by symbolizing celestial spheres and suggesting landscapes, rivers, skies, and cloud forms that are united by the central column, which represents a ladder reaching to the heavens.

Main entrance
St. Andrew the Apostle Catholic Church, Gibbsboro, New Jersey
7ft. by 25ft. (5.2m by 7.6m)
James B. Furman 1991

"MY STYLE IS ABSTRACT AND CONTEMPORARY, BUT HAS ITS ROOTS IN THE THOUSAND-YEAR-OLD TRADITION OF GLASS AND LEAD. I FAVOR A CONSTRUCTIVIST, BUILT APPEARANCE THAT EXPRESSES ITSELF THROUGH THE USE OF LAYERS OF GLASS AND OTHER MATERIALS SUCH AS METALS AND STONE. THE LEAD LINE IS ALSO VERY IMPORTANT AND I MAKE NO ATTEMPT TO HIDE OR SUBVERT IT. THIS RESULTS IN A WINDOW OR PANEL THAT IS OFTEN SCULPTURAL IN FEELING."

DANIELA GRANZIN

Daniela Granzin's glass screen, *25 Panels*, was part of her degree show at the West Surrey College of Art and Design, England, and now stands in an architect's office in Berlin. Each of the panels is a piece of float glass with a system of abstract and geometrical designs sandblasted, acid etched and enameled on to the surface. The panels have then been suspended within a steel grid framework and left free to swing, creating constantly shifting patterns of light and shadow. Much of Granzin's current work uses methods of casting into sand and metal molds to form bricks of glass. From these she creates decorative glass walls and internal screens which divide a space while still allowing light through.

25 Panels

Screen, Berlin, Germany
6¼ft. by 5¼ft. (1.9m by 1.6m)

Daniela Granzin 1991

THE PIECES I CREATE ARE CONCERNED WITH SPECIFIC ARCHITECTURAL SPACES, WORKING WITH BOTH NATURAL AND ARTIFICIAL LIGHT. GLASS IS BOTH A MATERIAL AND A MEDIUM BY WHICH LIGHT IS TRAPPED AND DIRECTED TO CREATE A SPACE WITHIN THE PIECE ITSELF. I AM INTERESTED IN THE FORMAL PLAY OF STRUCTURED AND CHANCE-BASED ELEMENTS THAT FORM GRIDS, RHYTHMS, POINTS AND MOVEMENT.

GÜNTER GROHS

Architectural glass artist Günter Grohs graduated in the late 1980s from the Halle Academy of Arts in the former East Germany. He then set up his own studio, conducting mainly experimental work since he was hampered by the lack of materials available in his country at that time. In recent years he has collaborated with several professional glass studios in Germany, designing windows and installations for churches, public buildings, and private collections in Europe and the United States. He specializes in antique, flashed, float, and fused glass, and his work is distinctive in its minimal use of lead, combined with expressive etching, painting, and use of silver stain. He prefers to work with a limited palette of colors because he feels "the eye needs resting places in a world of advertising," so in a single window he may use only two or three colors.

Main window behind the altar
St. Michael's Church, Volkershausen, Germany
Günter Grohs 1992

"THE ARCHITECTURE PRIMARILY DETERMINES THE STAINED-GLASS DESIGN BUT EACH ROOM WITHIN A BUILDING INSPIRES ITS OWN WINDOW. I SEE THE GLASS AREA ITSELF AS A LIGHT FILTER THAT ALLOWS US TO VIEW THE OUTSIDE, SHOWING THE WORLD AROUND US."

RENATE GROß

The surreal appearance of a giant wall of water cascading down the side of a building is the result of a remarkable piece by Renate Groß. In contrast to her previous works, which used sheets of antique glass, this was her first large-scale commission painting on float glass—a field in which she is now considered a pioneer. Finding a way to handle and paint such large pieces of glass was an exciting challenge for Groß, eventually enabling her to paint freely and expressively over large areas. Sheets of sandblasted float glass were drawn on with wax and enamel crayons, then painted and airbrushed before being fired in a kiln to toughen the glass and fix the enamels. Finally, rectangular areas of text— shadow words—and Helmhof motifs were sandblasted into the colored surface, providing formal structure among the otherwise fluid imagery.

Window wall

Helmhof building, Gersthofen, Bavaria
1,300 sq. ft. (120m²)
Renate Groß 1994

FLOAT GLASS IS IN COMPLETE CONTRAST TO ANTIQUE GLASS BECAUSE THE SURFACE IS COMPLETELY FLAT AND ONE SHEET IS LIKE ANOTHER, SO THE ARTIST HAS TO BRING HER OWN EXCITEMENT TO THE GLASS.

DOUGLAS HOGG

Glass artist Douglas Hogg has been commissioned to produce numerous windows, particularly for churches, and since the early 1970s has been involved in a succession of major exhibitions. Hogg is head of the Architectural Glass department at Edinburgh College of Art, Scotland, where he was once a student of painting and stained glass. Now working principally as a glass painter, Hogg uses light and color to communicate personal statements often inspired by dramatic landscapes, metaphors and poetic ideas. The expressive and potent use of dark iron oxide paint in conjunction with the vivid colors of enamels and silver staining are characteristic of much of Hogg's work, along with a sculptural use of lead. In *We Wait for Light*, beaten and seamed lead sheet is used as the base for a matrix of glass squares inscribed with Gothic script and gilded with gold leaf.

We Wait for Light

First exhibited at the British Crafts Council, London, England

Douglas Hogg 1997

"THE GOTHIC SCRIPT SHOWN IN IN THIS PIECE OF WORK HAS REFERENCES TO THE 8TH-CENTURY COURT OF CONSTANTINE THE GREAT, WHERE THE SCRIBE, PUBLILIUS OPTATIANUS PORFYRIUS ARRANGED HIS WORDS IN A VISUALLY INTERESTING WAY, SO AS TO CREATE VISUAL AS WELL AS VERBAL POETRY."

In addition to her commissioned work, which ranges from restoration to ornate screens, panels, and site-specific individual pieces, glass artist Shirley How has developed a range of unique mirrors that she supplies to selected stores and galleries. Inspired by an eclectic mixture of Native American, Art Nouveau, and Gothic styles, the mirrors combine shed snakeskins and the traditions of leaded glass. In the range of works entitled *Reptile Reflections*, How traps the delicate skins of Burmese pythons and other snakes between two layers of clear glass, which together are placed into one lead came—a process called plating—to form a decorative frame surrounding the mirrors. Once laminated, the intricate patterns of the fragile papery sloughs are revealed and protected.

Detail of *Snake Frame*

From the *Reptile Reflections* range, exhibited at Himley Hall, Himley, West Midlands, England
23in. by 54in. (57.5cm by 135cm)
Shirley How 1997

THE SNAKESKINS VARY GREATLY IN APPEARANCE, FROM THE LACELIKE TRANSPARENCY OF THE ALBINO TO THE DARK MOSAIC PATTERNS OF THE PYTHON AND THE SUBTLE COLORS OF THE CORN SNAKE.

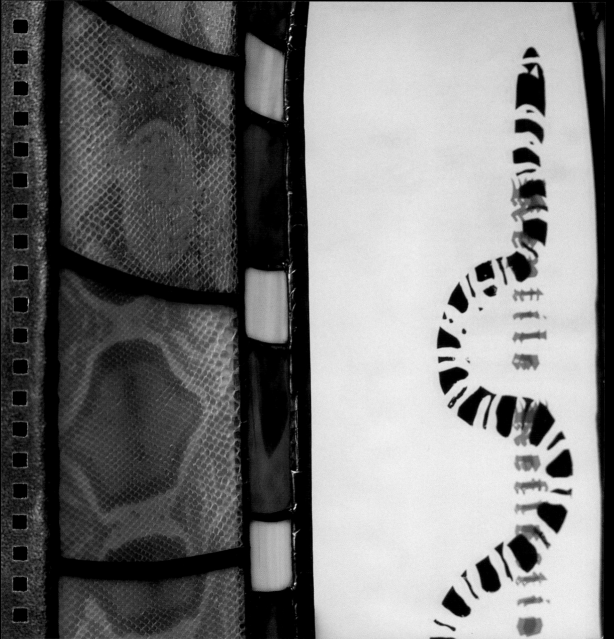

LAURA JOHNSTON

The interaction between glass, light, and space is Johnston's prime concern when designing. The influence of glass on an internal space by reflecting, transmitting, refracting, and filtering light is paramount. In her work *Shoal* at the National Glass Centre in Sunderland, 80 pieces of dichroic glass, 3¼ft. (1m) long, are suspended at varying heights and angles from the glass roof, creating a free-flowing form that sweeps throughout the interior of the building. In the design stages she worked closely with the engineers and architects to decide the exact positioning of the glass and constructed a model of the building to analyze the fall of natural light and help determine the most dramatic effects dichroic glass could have within the building.

Detail of *Shoal: An Exploration of Light, Color, and Liquid Space*

Commissioned by the National Glass Centre, Sunderland, England

Laura Johnston 1998

THE INTERIOR OF THE BUILDING IS ANIMATED WITH AN EVER-CHANGING PLAY OF LIGHT AND COLOR DURING THE COURSE OF THE DAY. THE SCULPTURE RESEMBLES A SHOAL OF FISH MOVING THROUGH SPACE AND, EVEN IN OVERCAST CONDITIONS, CONSTANTLY CHANGES COLOR DEPENDING ON THE ANGLE FROM WHICH IT IS VIEWED.

KESHAVA (ANTONIO L. SAINZ)

The vast glass mural *El Despertar Del Planeta* transforms the main entrance hall of an office building in Barcelona. This colossal piece has a dramatic impact on both the interior and exterior space. The work measures 82ft. by 72ft. (25m by 22m) and consists of 7 tons of toughened float glass, acid etched with an image of the awakening earth. It is complemented by the mobile sculpture *El Eclipse Permanente*, nearly 16½ft. (5m) in diameter, which is suspended from cables over the reception desk and designed to create a continuous solar eclipse. The movement of the sculpture is controlled by computer so that it follows the sun's trajectory, screening the area from the sun's rays. Details of colored glass and optical glass prisms are attached to both works using silicone glues.

El Despertar Del Planeta (The Awakening of the Planet), and *El Eclipse Permanente (The Permanent Eclipse)*

Glass mural and mobile sculpture. Avda. Diagonal, Barcelona, Spain

Keshava (Antonio L. Sainz) 1993

MY AIM IS TO HUMANIZE MASSIVE GLASS ARCHITECTURE BY OFFERING A REMARKABLE ELEMENT THAT IS BOTH UNUSUAL AND ATTRACTIVE. THE ART WORK ALLOWS THE INTERIOR SPACE OF A BUILDING TO BE TRANFORMED, CREATING AN ATMOSPHERE WITH A HIGH CHROMATIC AND VISUAL VALUE.

RAY KING

Glass artist Ray King's glass work is characterized by the use of multiple flat-glass elements—particularly dichroic glass and float glass laminated with holographic film. These are suspended by stainless steel cables and rods to form spectacular geometrical shapes, inspired by natural forms and phenomena. His sculpture, *Light Wave,* at Rowan College in New Jersey resembles a giant DNA molecule. Four 46ft (14m) helices, composed of an array of 4ft- (1.2m) long laminated glass bars, are threaded on to tensioned cables which stretch across the library reading room. Holographic film laminated within the glass produces vivid chromatic colors that alter as the observer moves.

Light Wave
Commissioned for the Library Reading Room, Rowan College of New Jersey
4ft. by 4ft. by 48ft. (1.2m by 1.2m by 14.6m)

Ray King 1994

MY WORK IS SYNTHETIC OF MANY AREAS OF INTEREST I HAVE IN THE DEVELOPMENT OF SCULPTURES THAT USE GLASS AND METALS TO CREATE AN ART WORK THAT KEEPS THE VIEWER CONTINUALLY OBSERVING THE NATURAL PHENOMENON OF LIGHT.

STEPHEN KNAPP

An established artist who works with a diverse range of materials including glass, metal, stone, and ceramics, Stephen Knapp has worked principally with architectural glass over the last decade, transforming sheets of float glass into highly textured internal walls, doors, furniture, and sculpture. Knapp works by first preparing a full-size drawing, then constructing a low-relief collage with a collection of mixed media such as cardboard, wood, and rope. This acts as a model, which is cast in a wet mixture of plaster, sand, and other heat-resistant materials. When the mixture has set, the model is removed, leaving a textured mold for the glass. In the kiln, the heat softens a sheet of clear or colored glass and the pattern of the mold is imparted to its surface.

Treasures

Wall of tempered kiln-formed art glass, commissioned by CNA Insurance Companies, Chicago, Ilinois
8½ft. by 18ft. (6m by 5.5m)
Stephen Knapp 1998

"LIGHT, COLOR, MOVEMENT—ALL SEEM TO MIGRATE TO PLAY ACROSS THE SURFACE OF THE GLASS, MAKING IT A KINETIC, VIBRANT MEDIUM. WHEN PEOPLE TELL ME WHAT THEY SEE IN AN INSTALLATION OF MINE—NIGHT SKY, FOSSILS, MOVEMENT, ARCHEOLOGY, TECHNOLOGY—ALL DIFFERENT, ALL VARIED, BRINGING THEIR OWN PERSPECTIVE TO MY WORK, THEN I HAVE SUCCEEDED."

DANNY LANE

American-born artist, Danny Lane has based himself in London since completing a degree in fine art at the city's Central School of Art and Crafts in 1980. He established an international reputation through his unique sculptural furniture made from stacked columns of float glass. This characteristic technique is now applied to towering sculptures and vast architectural installations, blurring the distinction between art and architecture. Lane regards his methodology as the application of industrial techniques and materials freed from their usual constraints and functions. The forceful handling of raw materials and the sheer scale of his work give a powerful sense of presence and inner energy.

Digital

Free-standing sculpture, commissioned for Digital Equipment Scotland Ltd, Edinburgh, Scotland
26ft. by 10ft. by 3ft. (8m by 3m by 0.9m)

Danny Lane 1991

IN THE SCULPTURE DIGITAL, I USE SANDBLASTED GLASS IN CONJUNCTION WITH FLOWING ORGANIC SHAPES OF FORGED STEEL TO EXPLORE METAPHYSICAL THEMES OF NATURE. HERE, PRIMITIVE HUMAN AND ANIMAL FORMS ARE REPRESENTED AGAINST A CENTRAL RING—HALF STEEL, EVOKING THE ELEMENTS OF FIRE AND EARTH; HALF GLASS, EVOKING AIR AND WATER—HELD IN BALANCE BY THE SNAKE THAT DEVOURS HIS OWN TAIL; THE CYCLE OF LIFE AND DEATH IN BALANCE—ENDLESS.

JON LEWIS

Glass-blower and stained-glass artist, Jon Lewis studied all forms of glass-making at University before going on to specialize in blowing at the International Glass Centre in Brierley Hill, England. His work is alive with humor, vivid designs, and vibrant colors, which are translated from simple drawings on paper into a more animated existence in glass. Working with techniques such as sandblasting, painting, staining, and brilliant-cutting, Lewis creates both abstract and figurative designs on a wide range of solid-colored and flashed antique glass, much of which he blows himself. As a commissioned artist he works closely with the client to produce a design that fulfills the design brief and enhances the surrounding environment.

Zebra Fish
Stained glass piece, sold privately
18in. by 14in. (46cm by 36cm)
Jon Lewis 1996

AS BOTH A GLASS-BLOWER AND A STAINED-GLASS ARTIST, THE CONTRAST BETWEEN THE INSTANTANEOUS RESULTS OF GLASS-BLOWING AND THE PROGRESSIVE SATISFACTION OF WORKING TOWARD THE COMPLETION OF A WINDOW IS ABLE TO BE ENJOYED.

ZEBRA
FISH

LINDA LITCHMAN

Color and light are the media that Linda Litchman works with; glass is the material and exploration is her method, as she seeks to expand on the palette of manufactured colors available in stained glass. Using a variety of subtractive and additive techniques, such as sandblasting, acid etching, and staining, she transforms solid-colored or flashed sheets of glass into a multitude of hues and textures. Litchman's other techniques include engraving as well as painting the glass with enamels that she scratches off when dry, creating playful, energetic lines and squiggles. Her windows and autonomous panels are either joined together using lead or bound with wires and suspended within a metal framework. Their motifs reflect images from nature—leaves, fish and, other natural forms and landscapes—"both the seen and the imagined."

Proposal for Emir's New Palace
11½in. by 21in. (29cm by 53cm)
Linda Litchman 1991

"GLASS CONTAINS WITHIN IT MANY CONTRADICTIONS. IT CONNECTS US TO, AND SEPARATES US FROM, THE WORLD. IT PROTECTS AND EXPOSES. GLASS CREATES A SEEMINGLY FRAGILE BOUNDARY THAT HOLDS BOTH THE MATERIAL AND THE IMMATERIAL."

PROPOSAL FOR THE FUTURE NEW PALACE

LL 1997

PAUL MARIONI AND
ANN TROUTNER

Since 1977, Paul Marioni and Ann Troutner have collaborated on more than 50 private and public commissions. Their aim is to create an interactive artwork that the people who use the facility or area can identify with. Troutner and Marioni have a particular affinity for cast glass, which they see as a timeless and elegant material that exacts few demands on its environment. They recommend cast glass as an ideal material for windows, walls, and entrances because of its light-transmitting qualities and its unique ability to capture, magnify, and manipulate light while obscuring the view. The commission _Waterwall_ is a cast-glass wall that divides a spa and an indoor swimming pool.

Waterwall

Cast glass. Commissioned for
a private residence.
6⅞ft. by 6ft. (2.1m by 1.8m)

Marioni & Troutner 1990

THE LIGHT QUALITY LOOKS REMARKABLY LIKE WATER AND CONTRIBUTES TO THE SERENE SETTING. WATER APPEARS TO FLOW OUT OF THE CEILING AND DISAPPEARS INTO THE FLOOR, CREATING A SURREAL STILLNESS.

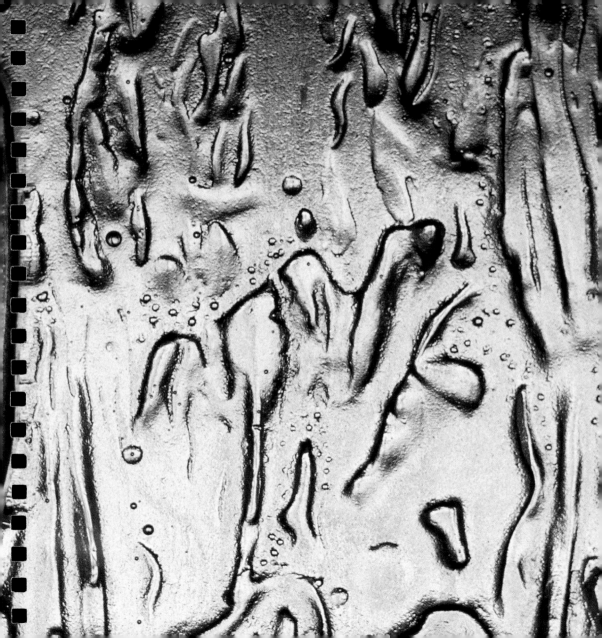

JANE MCDONALD

In addition to her exhibitions and private work, Jane McDonald has worked on numerous public commissions and is an experienced teacher. McDonald has developed innovative techniques for working with sheets of toughened and laminated glass, which enable her to construct large-scale work without relying on traditional methods of assembly. During the toughening process she decorates flashed or clear glass with metallic lusters, creating vivid iridescent colors. The density of color is then reduced in some places by sandblasting and etching, leaving a lighter, more transparent appearance. Much of her work is constructed out of two pieces of toughened glass laminated together to form a double-glazed unit. This protects the delicate lusters on the inner surfaces of the glass and gives a greater visual depth because the colors and images are overlaid.

Glass wall
Proposal for the atrium of the Empire Theatre, Liverpool, England
Jane McDonald 1998

INITIAL IDEAS WERE BASED ON DRAWINGS OF BIRDS' FEATHERS. THROUGH PLAYING WITH SCALE AND VISUAL DEPTH A SENSE OF DRAMA WAS ACHIEVED FOR THIS PROPOSAL, WHICH IS INTENDED FOR A THEATER. LAYERS OF COLOR WERE APPLIED AND ABRADED BY SANDBLASTING AND ACID ETCHING, GIVING THE GLASS A COMPLEX SURFACE.

JERA MAY MORTON

Jera May Morton works as a sculptor principally in glass, which she combines with various other materials, both natural and synthetic. Clay models infused with found objects create life-size figures that—through a series of lengthy mold-making stages—are transformed into glass. Often only the head or some focal point of the body is made from glass and the rest is fashioned out of other materials. For *Green Christ*, float glass was screen printed with a mixture of enamels and metallic powders, creating a deep green textured surface. Once fired, the glass was sandblasted and worked on using pencils, inks, and oil colors. The piece is leaded within a framework of steel rods and adorned with tendrils of ivy.

Green Christ
Commissioned by St. James' Church, Piccadilly, London
6ft. by 3ft. (1.8m by 0.9m)
Jera May Morton 1992

I AM CONSTANTLY DRAWN BY THE IMMENSE SCOPE KILN-FORMED GLASS AFFORDS TO ADAPT ANCIENT TECHNIQUES OR INVENT NEW ONES, ENABLING ME TO BE CREATIVELY INVOLVED AT BOTH THE TECHNICAL AND DESIGN STAGES.

STEVEN NEWELL

After obtaining a degree in Ceramics and Glass, the American-born artist Steven Newell went on to study at the Royal College of Art in London, and has since lived and worked principally in England. On leaving the Royal Collage, he joined The Glasshouse, a blown-glass workshop in Covent Garden, and later became a director. He is well known for his large blown plates and bowls characterized by stylized figures and animals that are etched or sandblasted into the colored surface. Newell's work is divided into two main strands: his repeatable items, which form part of the Newell Glass range, and his highly personal individual pieces, which are regularly exhibited internationally. Other work includes his privately and publicly commissioned works, particularly in stained glass, and cast glass, and his large installations.

With Care

Sheet glass, stained, painted, sandblasted, and leaded. Commissioned by Boots The Chemists, Nottingham, England

Steven Newell 1993

WITH CARE REPRESENTS THE TRIANGLE OF RESPONSIBILITY BETWEEN THE COMPANY, THE EMPLOYEES, AND THE CUSTOMER. IT ALSO REFERS TO THE TERM 'HANDLE WITH CARE', BRINGING IN THE FRAGILITY OF THE RELATIONSHIP AND OF THE MATERIAL.

REBECCA NEWNHAM

Using the ancient technique of
mosaic, Rebecca Newnham creates
works in two and three
dimensions for the private and
public sectors. She applies her
skills in a variety of different
contexts, from site-specific
artwork to garden fountains,
private fireplaces, bathroom wall
panels, and floors. She also creates
mosaic furniture, sculpture, and a
range of mirrors that are sold
internationally. The three-
dimensional elements in her work
are constructed from fiberglass,
wood, or concrete and covered
with tiny glass tesserae. The deep
colors are obtained either by
painting onto clear glass with
enamels and then firing it or by
gilding the glass with gold, silver,
or copper leaf.

Frisco

Convex mirror with mirrored mosaic,
sold privately.
31½in. (80cm) in diameter

Rebecca Newnham 1995

**FRISCO IS A DEVELOPMENT FROM EARLIER WORK WHICH
AIMS TO MAXIMISE THE BEAUTY OF GLASS MOSAIC BY
PRESENTING THE MIRROR WITH SIMPLICITY AND IMPACT.**

FELICE NITTOLO

The Italian artist Felice Nittolo applies his skills in ceramics, painting, drawing, and sculpture to the ancient craft of mosaic. A professor and pioneer of contemporary mosaic at the State Institute of Art in Ravenna, Italy, he is continually broadening the many possibilities of his medium, which he promotes as a "new tradition." Using cardboard, plastics, and acrylic resins as a support and base for the mosaic, Nittolo creates pillars, arches, cones, spheres, and other sculptural forms. He also paints in mosaic and covers floors, walls, ornaments and even everyday items such as chairs and shoes with his tesserae. In much of his work, Nittolo combines the traditional materials of glass, enamels, and marble tesserae with fired brick, mirrored glass, metals, wood, and fragments of seashells.

If there were no wars, the world would be golden

Glass mosaic in gold and silver
46in. (118cm) in diameter

Felice Nittolo 1993

THE CUBIC TESSERAE FIND IN THE ROUND SURFACE THE BEST ENHANCEMENT TO THEIR COLOR AND GLASSY BRILLIANCE. SO, TO TAKE IN THE WORK ONE SHOULD LOOK NOT JUST AT THE SURFACE, BUT MUST ALSO LOOK AT THE LIGHT, AT THE VIBRANT COLOR OF PERCEPTION.

DAVID PEARL

Working principally with glass, the British artist David Pearl creates site-specific art for architecture. Having studied fine art in Toronto and architectural glass in Swansea, Wales, he began his freelance career in Wales, later establishing a second studio in Toronto. He has lectured, exhibited, and worked with other artists, poets, and architects on many commissions on both sides of the Atlantic. *Inserted Landscape* is a collaboration with the landscape architect Ian Gray for the Canadian Clay and Glass Gallery in Waterloo, Ontario. The piece is in the form of a silo made almost entirely of glass, representing elements of both the rural and urban landscape. Layers of float glass, some of them overlaid with dichroic glass, are inscribed with maps and texts relating to the history of the site, expressing the past, present, and possible future of the landscape.

Inserted Landscape
For the Canadian Clay and Glass Gallery, Waterloo, Ontario
David Pearl and Ian Gray 1996–97

THE WORK IS AN EXAMPLE OF ART THAT ACTS AS INTERMEDIARY BETWEEN HUMAN PRESENCE AND ARCHITECTURE. IT IS CAREFULLY CONCEIVED TO INVOKE A SENSE OF PLACE—REFLECTING THE NATURAL AND HUMAN HISTORY OF THE SITE—AND ALSO TO BE A STAGE BETWEEN HUMAN AND ARCHITECTURAL SCALE. THE GLASS IS LIKE A LENS LOOKING THROUGH THE PRESENT TO THE PAST.

DAVID PRYTHERCH

A teacher of sculpture by training, David Prytherch is well known for his sculptural blown and deeply carved glass, for which he has designed and made his own specialized tools. Architectural glass and its accompanying restrictions provide a fascinating challenge for Prytherch, to which he frequently returns. The two windows for the Broadfield House Glass Museum are based on the physical feelings and emotional involvement of working with such a difficult medium. One of the windows is concerned with controlling and manipulating hot glass, the other with cold working. In *The Hot Window* three figures are dish-cut into float glass using a diamond wheel cutter. There are also a number of blown elements glued onto the face of the windows, along with thin sheets of antique glass and some old glass rescued from a local church.

Glass Dance

The Hot Window, commissioned by Broadfield House Glass Museum, Stourbridge, England

David Prytherch 1994

THE BLOWN PIECE THAT THE MAIN FIGURE CARRIES ON HIS/HER IRON IS ENGRAVED WITH THE JUGGLER FROM *THE COLD WINDOW*, RE-ESTABLISHING THE CONNECTIONS BETWEEN WHAT MIGHT FIRST APPEAR TO BE DISPARATE APPROACHES TO THE MATERIAL. THIS JUGGLER IS, IN A WAY, MY SIGNATURE SINCE AS WELL AS A FEW BALLS, HE IS JUGGLING VARIOUS OTHER OBJECTS THAT SYMBOLIZE THE MANY THINGS I JUGGLE WITHIIN MY DAY-TO-DAY LIFE.

JOHANNES SCHREITER

The unorthodox use of lead and the purity of his ideas have singled out Johannes Schreiter as a contemporary pioneer of stained glass whose original and controversial approach has influenced many other artists in his field. Schreiter insists that the lead cames are worked exactly according to his cartoon and consequently they have an organic and spontaneous appearance—meandering in all directions, sometimes torn and jagged, tapering off or abruptly ending in the middle of a piece of glass. Schreiter is also one of the few artists who combine Plexiglass with glass and lead, often featuring it as an opaque white background to emphasize the dynamic lines of lead across its surface.

Detail from a large window wall
St. Bernhard's Church, Münster, Westfalen, Germany
Johannes Schreiter 1997

THE LARGE WINDOW WALLS DEPICT PILLARS OF DIFFERENT HEIGHTS AND FUNCTIONS AS SYMBOLS OF STEADFASTNESS, REPRESENTING MARTIN LUTHER'S WORDS EXPRESSING THE INDISPENSABILITY OF PRAYER; "CHRISTIANS WHO PRAY ARE LIKE PILLARS, WHO CARRY THE ROOF OF THE WORLD."

BRONSON SHAW

The challenge of a new design provides the Spanish artist Bronson Shaw with enough energy and motivation to create vast works in architectural glass, such as the market building commission in Amposta, Spain. The work consists of 56 leaded, colored-glass windows—the majority 13ft. (4m) high and more than 3ft. (1m) wide—and has taken over four years to make. The concept for the main façade was to replace the old and damaged windows with a homage to the bird life in the delta of the Ebro River. The remaining windows portray the surrounding rice fields against a backdrop of the prominent local mountains. Shaw has applied his knowledge of different types of glass to his artistic representation, using, for instance, beautiful iridescent glasses to show the fields in their glistening waterlogged state.

West windows

Central Market, Amposta,
Catalonia, Spain

Bronson Shaw 1997

"MY OBJECTIVE TO SHOCK THE VIEWER WITH HARMONY IS AKIN TO THE EXPERIENCES IN LIFE WHEN WE ARE SHOCKED BY AN ASPECT OF BEAUTY IN NATURE OR A PHRASE IN A BOOK OR A WORK OF ART. THE HARMONY CAN CONTAIN TENSIONS, DRAMAS, COLORS, LEAD LINES SHOOTING HERE AND THERE, BUT THE INTENTION AND THE DESIRED RESULT IS HARMONY."

RAQUEL STOLARSKI-ASSAEL

Through continuous exploration of ideas and experimentation with flat glass over 18 years, the Mexican artist Raquel Stolarski-Assael has developed a personal style in both technical and conceptual aspects. She works mainly by layering thick sheets of float glass, which she laminates using a specialist glass glue, to create the required volume for the piece. Each layer is sandblasted to sculpt the glass carving deeply into it and creating a textured surface. After blasting, the mat glass is acid treated to restore it to a transparent state. Stolarski-Assael then colors the sand-carved surface using inks and oil, acrylic and enamel paints, which are fixed with a coat of clear varnish. In much of her work she laminates pieces of colored glass or other flat materials such as metals, paper, bark, and feathers within the glass.

Guardian

41in. by 27½in. by 14in.
(105cm by 70cm by 36cm)
Raquel Stolarski-Assael 1998

SYMBOLS, MYTHS, AND ANCIENT CULTURAL ARCHETYPES PLAY A MAJOR ROLE IN MY WORK. I SEEK TO CONVEY A MESSAGE BY ADDRESSING A RANGE OF IDEAS, EMOTIONS, AND LONGINGS, BE IT THROUGH FIGURATIVE IMAGERY OR ABSTRACT DESIGN.

TOSHIO TAKAMI

The Japanese artist Toshio Takami works with architectural glass in corporate buildings and for private collectors. He has entered numerous competitions and received awards in both stained glass and the applied fine arts. He works with an interesting mix of antique glass, beveled pencils, or circles of glass with faceted jewel glass, prisms, and roundels. These are assembled with an artistic use of lead, combining geometrical patterns with meandering abstract lines as if drawn on the glass with a pencil. Using an amalgam of figurative and graphic designs, Takami expresses his thoughts and feelings about humankind, the future for the earth, and his appraisal of nature.

Sun Rise

Mr. Akashi's residence,
Kurume-city, Japan
5¼ft. by 7¼ft. (1.6m by 2.2m)
Toshio Takami 1997

THIS PIECE SHOWS THE SUN RISING FROM THE DARKNESS USING THE TRADITIONAL IMAGE OF JAPANESE LANDSCAPE PAINTING, IN WHICH ALL CREATURES AWAKE AND START NEW ACTIVITIES SURROUNDED BY CLEAN AIR, BREATHING TREES, AND QUIETLY FLOATING CLOUDS IN A WORLD OF ELEGANT SIMPLICITY. THE BEGINNING OF ANOTHER DAY.

KARL HEINZ TRAUT

By careful consideration of the location of a piece and the function and design of the building, architectural glass artist Karl Traut seeks to integrate his artwork completely into its environment, uniting it with the surrounding architecture. Traut uses a wide selection of antique and float glass, in clear, translucent, flashed, or opaque forms, which he works on with techniques such as sandblasting, acid etching, and enamel painting. In the church window shown here, he has created a tight grid in an opaque flashed glass. In each square a letter has been sandblasted out of the flashed glass; together the letters form the text of the Sermon on the Mount. The skilled intricacy of the lead work in this piece is quite remarkable.

Chancel Window

Matthäus Church, Wiesbaden, Germany
17ft. by 25½ft. (5.2m by 7.8m)
Karl Heinz Traut 1990

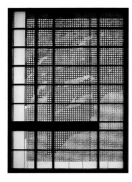

THE ARCHITECTURE OF THIS CHURCH CONVINCES THROUGH ITS CLARITY AND PRECISION, GOOD PROPORTIONS, AND BEAUTIFUL LIGHT CONDITIONS. THIS IS WHY I DECIDED THAT MY DESIGN SHOULD BE CLEAR AND PRECISE.

PERE VALLDEPÉREZ

The auditorium in Las Palmas in the Canary Islands houses a spectacular skylight designed by the Spanish artist Pere Valldepérez. This ambitious work consists of 2,150 sq. ft. (200m²) of stained glass and weighs 12 tons. A total of 36 glass pyramids held in a metal framework grow progressively larger, from 3¼ft. (1m) to 12½ft. (3.8m) in height. To symbolize the morning sun and solar magma, reflective glass has been used for the sloping faces, with an assembly of deep golden, yellow, red, and umber glasses—accurately cut and laminated between triangles of clear glass—for the vertical faces. Valldepérez teaches at the Massana School of Art in Barcelona. He has also restored some of Barcelona's most prestigious windows.

Skylight

Alfredo Klaus Auditorium, Las Palmas, Grand Canary

Pere Valldepérez 1997

I HAVE ALWAYS LIKED TO BECOME FAMILIAR WITH THE PLACE WHERE THE WINDOW IS TO BE PLACED. I MAKE SEVERAL VISITS AT DIFFERENT TIMES OF THE DAY SO THE PLACING OF THE WINDOW IS PERFECT.

MARY VAN CLINE

The American artist Mary Van Cline first started to combine glass with the medium of photography in 1980. Working with photosensitive glass and sandblasting resists, blown glass, cast glass, and neon, Van Cline creates sculptures and installations to transcend the restrictions imposed by our perception of the passage of time, existing purely in the present moment, without past or imagined future. Functioning on many levels, her work is rich with symbols of movement, time, and transformation, such as ladders, clocks, sundials, and hourglasses. The form of a house, a window, or a chair provides observers with a familiar standpoint as they enter a place where time is suspended, where figures and landscapes are captured in a moment and preserved through photography.

Linear Barriers

Pâte de verre and photosensitive glass
24in. by 14in. by 6in. (61cm by 35cm by 15cm)

Mary Van Cline 1997

 THE PHOTOGRAPHY COMMEMORATES ONE SINGLE MOMENT AND PRESERVES IT IN GLASS AND SCULPTURE, TRANSCENDING THE CONSTRAINTS OF TIME AS WE KNOW IT, TO MOVE BEYOND; "FORWARD AND BACKWARD."

SASHA WARD

Having initially obtained a degree in fine art, Sasha Ward graduated in 1985 from the Royal College of Art in London with an MA in Glass. Since then she has completed over 20 commissions in public buildings. Her main technique is hand-painting on glass, which she uses in combination with screen printing, sandblasting, and acid etching to create large fired and toughened panels of colored glass. The commission for the Edinburgh Court is screen printed and handpainted with many layers of overlapping color using a mixture of transparent and opaque enamels, silver stain, and iron oxide. Each pane of glass measures about 5ft. by 2½ft. (1.5m by 0.8m) and is attached to vertical glazing bars with hinges and locks.

Interior screen

Three of 14 panels. Commissioned by Edinburgh Sheriff Court, Scotland
5½ft. by 39ft. (1.7m by 12m)

Sasha Ward 1995

I THOUGHT OF THIS SCREEN, WHICH RUNS ALONG THE LENGTH OF A GLAZED WALL ON THE THIRD FLOOR OF THE BUILDING, AS A GIANT WATERCOLOR. THE PAINTED LANDSCAPE DEPICTS THE LOCAL AREA, CHARACTERIZED BY OLD AND NEW HOUSES, ROADS AND RAILWAYS, HILLSIDES AND ROCKY CRAGS.

Since obtaining an MA in Glass at the Royal College of Art, London, Sue Woolhouse has exhibited internationally, received a number of major public commissions, and completed a three year artist residency in Sunderland, England. Her work combines traditional leading with the unusual practice of imprinting natural objects into the glass. Woolhouse presses a flower or leaf into a bed of clay and then removes it, leaving an embossed image. She takes a wax model from the clay which, when cast in a heat-resistant cement, provides a mold for the glass. As the glass softens into the mold, it picks up even the finest detail, leaving an accurate impression of the flower or leaf. She then uses lead to join the kiln-formed panel to etched flashed or painted glass and jewels of faceted glass.

Daffodils

One of 16 panels based on "Seasons of the Year". Commission for Durham Aged Mineworkers Homes, Sunderland, England 8in. sq. (20m²)

Sue Woolhouse 1996

DAFFODILS IS ONE OF SIXTEEN PIECES BASED ON THE SEASONS OF THE YEAR. MY CHIEF CONCERN IN USING GLASS IS TO BE ABLE TO PAINT WITH LIGHT. IN THIS WAY, COLOR BECOMES A HEALING ELEMENT.

DANA ZAMECNIKOVA

The Czech artist Dana Zamecnikova is internationally renowned for her unique approach to flat glass. With an academic background in architecture and stage design, she began her career at the Prague National Theater. Influences from theater design and her use of perspective are especially apparent in her early glass work using layers of float glass. On each layer, part of the figure or image is sandblasted, painted, acid etched, or expressively applied with colored pencils. As the layers are positioned one behind another a single picture is created, often depicting a scene dramatized from life experiences and personal observations.

Conversation with Dog—Memory
Float glass, mixed media
Dana Zamecnikova 1998

THE SYMBOLS AND SIGNS IN MY WORK ARE BOTH GENTLE AND KIND, BUT ALSO NERVOUS AND BRUTAL. TOGETHER, THEY REFLECT THE ENIGMA OF MAN'S INNER BEING.

ACID ETCHING The use of a powerful acid to dissolve the surface of glass, leaving a smooth matt finish.

ANNEALING The gradual cooling of glass in a kiln to prevent cracking.

BEVEL An angle ground and polished in the edge of glass.

BLOWING IRON A hollow steel tube used in glass blowing.

BRILLIANT CUTTING The use of rotating abrasive wheels to make V-shaped cuts into the surface of glass.

CARTOON A scale drawing of the design for a stained-glass window

CASTING The melting of glass in a kiln so that it flows into a mold, or the pouring of hot glass from the furnace into a mold.

CROWN GLASS A flat disc of glass made by spinning an opened bubble of hot blown glass on a blowing iron.

CULLET Chunks of irregularly shaped glass used for kiln casting and re-melting in a new batch of glass.

DALLE DE VERRE A now little used method of embedding thick slabs of glass into an epoxy resin cement for use in windows.

DICHROIC GLASS A modern, metal-oxide coated glass, which shows opposite colors in reflected and transmitted light.

ENAMELS GLASS paints made from finely powdered glass combined with metal oxides which produce specific colors when fired onto the glass.

FLASHED GLASS A clear or colored glass thinly encased by two or more layers of glass of a contrasting color.

FLOAT GLASS A modern, mass-produced window glass made by floating molten glass onto a bed of molten tin.

FRIT Small fragments or granules of clear or coloured glass specifically made for use in kiln-forming techniques.

FUSING The union of separate pieces of glass by heating them in a kiln to the point that they soften and join together.

IRON A steel rod or tube used in glass-blowing procedures.

LAMINATED GLASS Flat glass composed of two or more layers joined together using a glass adhesive.

LEAD cames (or calmes) Strips of H-section lead used for joining pieces of flat glass in a stained-glass window.

LEHR A special kiln used to anneal glass, cooling the glass slowly to prevent cracking.

LENSES Circular domed glass lenses used as decorative elements in stained glass.

LUSTERS Glass paints containing metal compounds which leave iridescent metallic colors on the glass when fired.

MATTING A technique of shading areas of stained glass with a black or brown iron oxide enamel.

MOUTH-BLOWN GLASS Glasswork made by manipulating a bubble of molten glass, blown on a blowing iron.

NORMAN SLAB GLASS Small flat sheets of mouth-blown glass made from a bubble of molten glass blown into a rectangular mold.

PLATING Securing two layers of glass into one lead came.

PARAISON The initial bubble of molten glass formed on the blowing iron.

PATE DE VERRE A technique in which a paste of colored crushed glass, mixed with a binder, is positioned in a mold and fused in the kiln.

PRISMS Polished prism-shaped cast glass used as decorative elements in stained glass.

RESISTS Materials used to mask off areas on glass to protect them from sandblasting and acid etching.

RODS Thin rods of clear or colored glass purpose made for a variety of kiln-forming and blowing techniques.

SANDBLASTING A method of abrading the glass surface using grit or sand suspended in a jet of compressed air.

SILK-SCREEN PRINTING A printing method using a fine mesh through which paint is squeezed.

SILVER STAIN Silver nitrate paste used for coloring the glass. When fired in the kiln, silver ions migrate into the glass, permanently staining it from lemon yellow to amber red.

SHARDS Thin fragments of glass used in glass blowing made by shattering a large blown bubble of clear or colored glass.

SLUMPING A bending method in which sheets of glass are heated in the kiln until they soften and sag into or over molds.

TRACING The painting of outlines and line details on stained glass using brown or black iron oxide enamels.

TOUGHENED OR TEMPERED GLASS A float glass which has been rapidly heated and cooled to strengthen it.

ARTISTS' ADDRESSES

Mark Angus BRITISH
144 North Road
Bath BA2 5DL
United Kingdom

Alexander Beleschenko BRITISH
43 Jersey Street
Hafod
Swansea
West Glamorgan SA1 2HF
United Kingdom

Jeff Bell BRITISH
Glass Casts
299 Haggerstone Road
London E8 4EN
United Kingdom

Philippa Beveridge BRITISH
c/del Carmen 71,4o2a
08001 Barcelona
Spain

Ed Carpenter AMERICAN
1812 N.W. 24th Avenue
Portland
Oregon 97210
United States

Dale Chihuly AMERICAN
Chihuly Studio
509 NE Northlake Way
Seattle
WA 98105
United States
Homesite: www.chihuly.com

John K. Clark BRITISH
11a Maxwell Drive
Glasgow G41 5DR
United Kingdom
Email: john@glasspainter.com
Homesite: www.glasspainter.com

Elizabeth Devereaux AMERICAN
Elizabeth Devereaux Architectural
Glass
2155b Park Avenue
Chico
California 95928
United States

Martin Donlin BRITISH
16 St Catherines
Wimborne Minster
Dorset BH21 1BE
United Kingdom

James B. Furman AMERICAN
James B. Furman Glass Studio
P.O. Box 722
27 West Main Street
Trumansburg
NY 14886
United States
Email: jbfglass@lightlink.com
Homesite:
www.lightlink.com/jbfglass/

Daniela Granzin BRITISH
12 Brockill Crescent
London SE4 2PT
United Kingdom

Günter Grohs GERMAN
Dipl. -Glasgestalter
Friedrichstrasse 119a
38855 Wernigerode
Germany

Renate Groß GERMAN
Blumenstr 62
D-82110 Germering
Germany

Douglas Hogg BRITISH
Loganlea
Main Street
Gordon
Berwickshire TD3 6JN
United Kingdom

Shirley How BRITISH
5 Clifton Street
Stourbridge
West Midlands DY8 3XR
United Kingdom

Laura Johnston BRITISH
Laura Johnston – Architectural Glass
8 Ravenswood Road
Newcastle-upon-Tyne NE6 5TU
United Kingdom

Keshava (Antonio L. Sainz) SPANISH
c/Consejo de ciento 111
08015 Barcelona
Spain
Email: keshava@arquired.es
Homesite:
www.arquired.es/users/keshava

Ray King AMERICAN
835 N. 3rd Street
Philadelphia
PA 19123
United States
Email: ray@rayking.nu

Stephen Knapp AMERICAN
74 Commodore Road
Worcester
MA 01602
United States
Homesite: www.stephenknapp.com

Danny Lane AMERICAN
19 Hythe Road
London NW10 6RT
United Kingdom

Jon Lewis BRITISH
Unit F4
The Chocolate Factory
Farleigh Place
London N16 7SX
United Kingdom

Linda Litchman AMERICAN
17 Tudor Street
Cambridge
MA 02139
United States

Paul Marioni and
Ann Troutner AMERICAN
4136 Meridian Avenue North
Seattle
Washington 98103
United States

Jane McDonald BRITISH
Jane McDonald Glass
3 Beechcroft
Dorchester-on-Thames
Wallingford
Oxfordshire OX10 7LS
United Kingdom

Jera May Morton BRITISH
'Geertje'
Canal Lock House 92
Windmill Lane
Norwood Green
Middlesex UB2 4NH
United Kingdom

Steven Newell AMERICAN
Newell Glass
Glass Works (London) Limited
12 Victoria Terrace
London N4 4DA
United Kingdom

Rebecca Newnham AMERICAN
Palmerston
Kingston
Ringwood BH24 3BG
United Kingdom

Felice Nittolo ITALIAN
Via A. Codronchi 61
48100 Ravenna
Italy
Email: fnittolo@racine.ravenna.it
Website: www.mosaic.it

David Pearl BRITISH
1 Greenfield Terrace
Sketty
Swansea
West Glamorgan SA2 9BS
United Kingdom

David Prytherch BRITISH
11 Brook Road
Oldswinford
Stourbridge
West Midlands DY8 1NQ
United Kingdom

Johannes Schreiter GERMAN
Rotkehlchenweg 7
D-63225 Langen
Germany

Bronson Shaw SPANISH
Camino Torre Vidal, s/n
(Medio Camino)
43500 Tortosa
(Tarragona)
Spain

Raquel Stolarski-Assael MEXICAN
MBosques de Tamarindos 17-1102
Col. Bosques de las Lomas
Mexico D.F. 05120
Mexico
Email: kolte@mail.internet.com.mx

Toshio Takami JAPANESE
Glass Art Takami
5-20-31 Tajima Jyonan-ku
Fukuokacity
Japan 814-0113

Karl Heinz Traut GERMAN
Parkstraße 18
D-65232 Taunusstein
Germany

Pere Valldepérez SPANISH
c/Alcalde de Mostoles 43
03025 Barcelona
Spain
Email: VALLDE@teleline.es

Mary Van Cline AMERICAN
P.O. Box 61313
Seattle
WA 98121
United States

Sasha Ward BRITISH
Sasha Ward Glass
19 Salisbury Road
Marlborough
Wiltshire SN8 4AD
United Kingdom

Sue Woolhouse BRITISH
Studio 3
Level 1
Ouseburn Warehouse Workshops
36 Lime Street
Newcastle-upon-Tyne NE1 2PN
United Kingdom

Dana Zamecnikova CZECH
Academy of Applied Arts
Stoduecka 209-11
15800 Prague 5
Czech Republic

INDEX

ACKNOWLEDGMENTS

The publishers would like to thank the following for the use of their photographs:

p113 David Bird

p123 Jed Colome

p135 Kate Gadsby
(By permission of the Sheriff Principal of Lothian and Borders)

p104, p105 Richard Margolis

p103 Bruce T. Martin

p67 Agusti Nubiola

p71 Terry Rishel/Dale Chihuly

p127 Yuji Shinomiya

p89 Richard Waite

p58, p98 Peter Wood

p79 Fabian Zimmerman

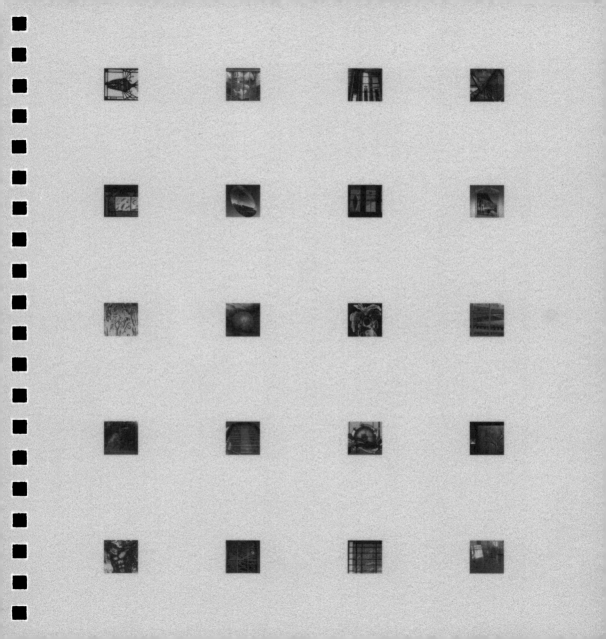